A MATTER OF
FAITH

LEN TITOW

SWEETSPIRE **LITERATURE**
——— MANAGEMENT ———

Notation

When it comes to religion most people think "divine" and the minister can do no wrong as he represents God.

The reality is that the Church and its ministry are just a reflection of society and as such has the good and bad characteristics found in our society, and in mankind generally.

Some would like you to think of the church and its ministry as representing the Divine, but unfortunately most of us fall short of this.

There are rotten apples in society as well as in the church and in the ministry. Ministers would deny this, but reality shows this to be the case. The book tries to demonstrate this by way of a number of stories and that the church should not hold itself out to be "holier than though" but be truthful and seek forgiveness, for they merely reflect society and sin like the rest of us.

My hope is that you maintain your faith in the God you believe in, and not in those who represent Him on this earth. That you will speak to God direct, through your' prays.

Those who fall by the wayside are mere men, who like you, can choose to follow Satin instead of God. There is little doubt that materiality is the key factor here.

Our criticism against the church or its ministry should not be any different to what transpires in society generally, when laws are broken. An attempt to smear religion because of the wrong doing of someone in the church is an attempt to discredit those who believe in God.

May you enjoy this book.

Len Titow

Apostles' Creed:

I believe in God, the Father almighty,
Creator of heaven and earth,
and in Jesus Christ, His only Son, our Lord,
who was conceived by the Holy Spirit,
born of the Virgin Mary,
suffered under Pontius Pilate,
was crucified, died, and was buried.
He descended into hell;
on the third day, He rose again from the dead.
He ascended in heaven
and sits at the right hand of God,
the Father almighty;
from thence, He shall come again
to judge the living and the dead.
I believe in the Holy Spirit,
the Holy Catholic Church,
the communion of saints,
the forgiveness of sins,
the resurrection of the body,
and life everlasting.
Amen.

I hope that scripture, which I believe is paramount to mankind's existence, is brought out in this book and that the issues raised lead to further discussion.

I thank the Lord for His inspiration and guidance in writing this book.

Chapter 1

It was a cold and miserable day. I looked at my watch. It showed 10:00 a.m. We were at the Northside Chapel. I came to see what type of send-off was going to be given to Russel Brown, a well-known businessperson, a politically influential and wealthy member of our community.

The sky was gray and bleak. For the last three days, the rain had been persistent and heavy. The wind twirled the rain around, making umbrellas useless. A crowd had gathered, and more were coming. Everyone was waiting for the hearse to arrive with the coffin while still trying to keep out of the rain. Some didn't bother and stood in the rain with their umbrellas up, nodding to politicians and the suit squad as they passed by.

Some of the elderly went inside the chapel and sat in the pew, waiting for the service to begin. Comments were made about the decor of the chapel and the flower arrangements. Then the discussion moved on about 'what a good man the deceased was', 'it is a pity he died suddenly', 'the good always go first', 'never thought his life would end so abruptly', and 'no doubt with his wealth, he has gone to heaven'.

Outside, the rain intensified, and you could hear the expectation that the hearse was not far away. The lead car pulled around the side of the chapel to let the family get out without interference from the crowd and to move into the chapel and take up their positions.

The hearse pulled up outside the entrance to the chapel, and four men got out of the car. They moved around the back of the hearse, opened the tailgate, and slid out of the coffin. They carried it into the chapel and put it on the stand in the front of the main hall so all could see the coffin. They gathered the flower display and placed them on the coffin, with the rest lying on the floor. In fact, there were too many flower arrangements. A lot had to be left in the entrance out of the rain. It seemed that all those who had dealt with Russel Brown had to send an expensive arrangement to ensure the family did not think they had anything but good thoughts about him.

The crowd moved behind the coffin as they brought it into the chapel and quickly filled the pews that were available. Politicians, business executives, and other influential people, both local and overseas, moved to their designated seats to ensure someone did not occupy them by mistake. The police took their positions outside the chapel entrance, and the commissioner moved to his seat at the front, alongside ex-premiers. TV commentators began their commentary, and the film crew named the rich and famous who had attended.

The family insisted on a minister of the church handling the service as they had contributed a lot towards the renovations of the church, and it would lend to the image of respectability. Peter Sutherland was chosen out of several candidates to perform the service, as he had known Russel for several years and was with him when he had died. The choir comprised an international tenor and two sopranos with six other singers. It seemed they were economizing as they used the piano that belonged to the chapel rather than bringing in a Yamaha.

They draped the coffin with expensive silk clothes. It had gold handles and an engraving on the top—'Rest in Peace'—with a gold cross on top. *A son that surely would go to heaven.*

I sat at the back of the chapel, listening to what they said. My name is Ray Brant and I am a reporter for the Daily newspaper. I was interested in the charade that is generally performed at these send-offs. I remember approaching a minister and asking him why don't you tell the families of

those being buried or cremated the truth—that their relative was not going to heaven, according to the Bible.

He replied, 'It's not our job to decide who goes to heaven or hell. That's God's job, not ours.'

There, I thought, *lies the problem. What a cop-out.*

Peter Sutherland began the service with a prayer and asked everyone to be seated. He described Russel Brown as a God-fearing man and one who had helped the church as and when called upon to do so. He described the generosity of the deceased, who was always ready to support worthwhile causes. He then introduced the next speaker, the brother of the deceased, who again described Russel in benevolent terms, emphasizing the good that was done as donations to various charities and causes. Nothing was said about how this money had been obtained or the rumours that continually were circulated about the dealings of Russel Brown and his family. Their criminality did not even get a mention.

I listened to the speeches and noted that everyone was saying Russel was a good man, God-fearing, and that he had gone to a better place. My mind drifted, and I thought, *Is this the same person I knew? Because if it is, he was no angel unless he bought a condominium in Lucifer's camp.*

I realized as usual, the nice things, the pleasantries, were being said, and these were not the truth. The man was not God-fearing. He believed in a different god – namely, Russel Brown – and used Christianity as a camouflage to ensure the appearance of respect and dignity. The church allowed him to gain respect under its influence. These days, to be able to pay money to influence people showed success, and with Russel, there were always takers.

While listening to what was being said, I continually found myself saying, *You hypocrite.* This was not a good man. He was an opportunist who took advantage of situations and was supported by politicians who sold him information at a price. *Go to heaven? You're joking. He will try to take control of hell.*

I knew they would not say here the truth as more speakers got up and praised Russel. I was waiting for the hand to appear and the writing on the wall to begin. *Of course, miracles don't happen these days.* It seemed that even the Lord was allowing this garbage to be said without a crack of thunder or lightning striking the coffin to advance the cremation process.

It baffled me why so many people came to funerals to hear what was predictable, and generally, the same garbage was said where there was wealth and influence involved. *Maybe they believe Russel will spill the beans to God on them to get to heaven. Or bribe the Lord for a free pass.* My mind was critical of the speakers and the lies they were willing to tell, and then it dawned upon me I could set the record straight by telling the truth in my article and not line up with the other hypocrites.

Unfortunately, reality dawned upon me I had a wife and two small kids to feed, and jobs were difficult to get, especially if you did the wrong thing towards one of the most powerful names in the state. They could make sure you starved and never found work. *I guess if I want to keep my job, I would have to report what I have seen and not the true facts.*

No. I am not a Christian. Nor do I believe in a God. Not when crooks like Russel Brown can get away with paying off the judiciary, police, and politicians and never seem to get brought to justice, yet the small man is fined for dropping a piece of paper in the street. It seems the amount of money or influence you have dictates justice.

One thing is for sure—justice is not something that is part of this world.

Chapter 2

Russel Brown was born into a wealthy family in a rich suburb. He went to a Christian school and ended up in one of the most prestigious universities, finishing a degree in economics, majoring in finance. His father got him a job with one of the leading bankers, and within several years, he became manager of retail banking. He was privy to information that not too many shareholders knew and had access to board minutes and details of potential acquisitions and expansions.

One day, he received a phone call from the CEO of Brolite Coal, a large public company listed on the stock exchange.

'Russel, we need to talk. The sooner, the better.'

Russel arranged a meeting for Tuesday at his office. This was attended by Phil Danulls and his CFO, Chris Brien.

Once the formalities were over and the door closed, Phil Danulls said, 'What we are about to tell you is extremely private information which is not to be stated outside this room. If our plan works out, we will make a takeover offer for Allied Coal. We intend to make a cash offer and will require the bank to arrange the funds.'

Russel asked, 'How much will you need?'

Phil explained, 'About four billion dollars. Here are the assessments of the deal and our evaluation of the acquisition. You are to begin work immediately in sourcing the funds for us as we need to know whether you can do this, and we need your answer within two weeks.'

Russel replied, 'I will do my best but cannot guarantee the bank will be able to borrow the full amount as quick as you expect. We will try, but I will need to inform the board so I can get support and the authority to act.'

Phil said, 'We are counting on you, and you are to speak to no one about what we have said.'

Russel nodded, and everyone stood up, and they all shook hands. He showed the men to the lift and returned to his office.

Russel arranged for a board meeting the next week and put the proposition to the board. He also advised them he had negotiated a fee of one hundred million dollars should the acquisition come off. The board unanimously supported the deal and gave Russel the right to handle the acquisition.

Russel began to put together a team who were to handle the acquisition and, shortly afterwards, concluded that a share and cash deal would be the better approach to take. He presented his recommendations to the board of Brolite Coal, who agreed with his approach. They set a date to advise the stock exchange of the pending takeover offer.

Russel approached Norms Accounting, an international accounting firm with connections in the Canary Islands. He had them establish an integrated maze of companies and borrowed a million dollars, which he used to acquire Brolite Coal shares in various trusts and fictitious names.

On the designated day, they handed an announcement to the stock exchange, and the shares of Brolite Coal quadrupled in price, and Russel became a billionaire overnight.

The Securities Commission had noted that there was a large number of shares acquired before the announcement of the acquisition and began to investigate, noting that an overseas buyer acquired the shares just before the announcement. They approached the bank to see if anyone knew anything about this, but everyone denied knowledge of it. Their investigations centered on a vast number of companies transacting the shares to one another, preventing the trace of the final owner. However, they could find that Russel had arranged for a million-dollar loan to his parent company prior to the announcement, and they homed in on him.

Russel denied knowledge of what he was accused of and declared client adviser privilege, which Securities Commission would not buy. They informed the board of the bank that they were being investigated by the Securities Commission and that they believed Russel had something to do with inside trading of the shares of Brolite. He knew he had to do something. Otherwise, he would find himself behind bars.

Jim Hydaburg was the federal minister for finance in the federal government. He had been an old school buddy of Russel's, and both kept in touch. Jim also had a daughter who had a unique strain of MS and who required constant medical treatment and support, which cost him a lot of money which he did not have. Also, Jim's farm was in drought, which meant he could not earn money from farming and grazing, and in fact, the farm was costing him money in that he had to try to maintain his breeding stock.

Russel approached Jim and advised him that the Securities Commission was investigating him for inside trading. Russel advised Jim that if he could help him, he was prepared to pay him two hundred thousand dollars, which would fix both their problems. Jim agreed and devised a plan to reduce the size of the budget of the Securities Commission as they were ineffective and over-staffed for the results achieved. He presented a plan to his cabinet meeting, which was adopted and carried by a majority. The plan called for the reduction of three thousand staff, which included the costly investigation unit. All staff were offered redundancy packages and were dismissed.

With his wealth intact, Russel acquired a building company that had gone into liquidation. He gathered a team of engineers and architects and submitted tenders but was unsuccessful in winning contracts. He went about the next tender differently. After scoping out his bid and submitting his tender, he invited all the senior executives of that firm to a party at one of Sydney's plush hotels. They all accepted his offer and, at night, were entertained with a lot of drink and entertainment. Most of the executives ended up sleeping with prostitutes and getting their pictures taken.

Russel held a meeting with the managing director of the firm the next morning and declared that he would release the pictures if he didn't win the tender. Russel succeeded and, using the same tactics time after time over the years, became a powerful force in the building and construction industry and a very wealthy man. Russel also acquired a restaurant and a brothel, which were used constantly to secure contracts and political favors.

To find respect, he decided to go to church every Sunday with his wife and children. The church he attended was old and in need of repairs, and he agreed to pay for its renovations 'to help God and the community'. The senior minister at St Andrew's Church was Peter Sutherland, who wanted a bigger, better, and more modern church, something that people would look up to as an icon and not a building from the medieval period.

Peter Sutherland, in his youth, believed in God and had faith. Over the years, he had forgotten about Jesus and the cross and had adopted an alternative god, one of the modern world in particular – the god of money and assets. Satan had entered him. Peter didn't care as he was achieving things that could be quantified and were visible, not spiritual and futuristic – things that he wanted. He was looking after number one, namely, himself.

To ensure that donations kept coming in, Peter preached justification through deeds rather than faith and that one's good deed ensured eternal life. Peter preached about material things and not spiritual and began to lose true believers.

Another minister at the church was Simon Fuller, who, contrary to Peter, had maintained his faith and had found himself constantly in conflict with Peter, whom Simon considered being an antichrist, not a genuine believer. Simon and Peter took the services on alternating Sundays to spread the workload. Simon preached justification by faith alone and not by deed, which conflicted with the church and, in particular, Peter's view.

The two came into conflict time after time on interpreting the Bible and the approach the church should take. It was not only Peter who seemed to preach contrary to the Bible but also other ministers who were employed there.

Simon could not understand what was going on and not just with Peter, but also it seemed the whole ministry in the dioceses had lost their faith and had allowed parishioners to wash away their sins by good deeds, which invariably meant a donation to the church.

The conflict was showing on Simon, who knew that if he wanted to keep his job, he would need to fall into line and do as he was told – follow modernity and not the teachings of Christ, as noted in the Bible.

Chapter 3

Simon came from an average working-class family in the suburbs. He was the only child. His father had died of cancer when he was 15, and his mother, a registered nurse, brought him up on her own. His mother went to church whenever she could, and Simon would go with her. She insisted he read the Bible and understand the Lord's Word.

He was an average student at school and enjoyed playing sports and hanging out with his mates whenever he could. He got a job at the local store when he was 15 to help his mother with the bills and stayed there until he went to theology college.

After high school, he went to college to become an accountant. In his first semester, he was standing at the lights to cross the road to get to class when a car sped out of control and headed straight for him. He froze and couldn't do anything. Just when the car was within twenty feet of him, another car came from the side street and collided with the out-of-control vehicle. Simon knew that this was a miracle and that the good Lord was looking after him. He knew he should dedicate his life to the Lord. He transferred to studying theology and became a minister once he graduated.

At university, Simon met his soon-to-be wife, Monique. She was a law student, and they fell in love and married shortly after he had graduated. Simon took up several positions after leaving university to gain experience and, after two years, was offered a position at St Andrews Church as a junior minister.

Monique graduated as a lawyer and took up a position with a medium-sized law firm. She found the work compromising in that the partners were telling clients how to avoid prosecution or avoid a large penalty by lying or cheating. She had to accept this situation as she was only a junior solicitor and the partners were the ones who gave the orders and not her. This lasted for about a year when she could not continue with the fraud being portrayed and was very uncomfortable with the decisions made by the firm.

One Tuesday morning, she came to work and was asked to draft an affidavit for a client stating lies. The client previously had instructed the firm, and the firm agreed they would defend an action on behalf of the client. Their defense was based on the fabrication of the evidence, with little truth in what was being said. It was designed to put the parties on a path where it was one person's word against the other.

Monique tried to tell herself that all she was doing was typing up the affidavit. She was not signing it, and she was not a party to the sham. She didn't draft it. Nor was she going to witness it. She didn't want to do it, as she knew this was wrong. She wasn't prepared to compromise her faith anymore and decided she would trust in the Lord. She said a brief prayer and went and spoke to her employer, who made it clear that there were quite a number of young people out of work with the same degree that she had. She would either do what was asked of her or leave the firm. She decided to stick to her principles and resigned from the firm.

She applied to other legal firms to get a job, but they wouldn't take her on once they had found out she wasn't prepared to do what was required of her, irrespective if it meant she had to attend to unethical dealings. She was prepared to represent criminals at court but would not lie for them. This also applied to businessmen who were trying to avoid paying taxes by interpreting a transaction or dealing in a way that would deem it legal when, in fact, it was anything but that.

Monique came from a family where her mother was a stay-at-home parent and looked after four kids. Her father was a bricklayer and would go to the pub after work to have drinks with his mates. The kids' upbringing was left to the mother, with the father attending to the yard and his work. They were not a religious family, but were always taught right from wrong. They never went to church as the father always thought it to be a waste of time dealing with a God that allowed the world to be in such a mess. Over the years, her father drank more alcohol and became an alcoholic and eventually died of sclerosis of the liver.

She finally got a job with the local library and stayed there until she was ready to give birth to her first child. Monique looked after her first child for a year and then went back to work, as they could not make ends meet. Her mother looked after her firstborn until he began preschool and then proper school. She worked for about eight years and then fell pregnant again. She stayed at work until two months before her second child was due to be born. Monique's second son was named Bill, who was disabled in that his oxygen supply was cut off during birth for a few minutes, which left the child brain-damaged and incapable of speech and with only partial movement of his arms and legs.

Simon lived in a rented house with his wife, Monique, and his two boys and yearned for the day when life would become easier and not a continual daily struggle. Simon and his wife both found it hard to come to terms with why God had done this to them and to Bill and for a long time believed it was the Lord punishing them for some sin in the past. After much prayer and consultation with members of the church, they had concluded that this was not the case, but part of God's well-developed plan.

They lived week to week and never seemed to get out of the 'pits of misery', and it seemed if ever they had gained a dollar, it vanished quickly on necessities. They believed the Lord would reveal His plan to them in good time and, in the meantime, held to their faith, but it was hard. The family struggled to make ends meet and keep up with the medical expenses for Bill.

Simon did not have many close friends as the congregation seemed to despise him in that he preached the Bible and not modernity, and they didn't believe they were getting value for money in that he preached that brimstone and fire would be the consequence if they deviated from the teachings of the Bible. They preferred Peter, who was less aggressive and did not take the one path of strict interpretation of the Bible.

Simon would not deviate from the Word of God as written in the Bible and found himself before the committee of elders frequently facing accusations which were brought against him in the 'star chamber'. His ministry wasn't bringing in the dollars that others seemed to do.

Chapter 4

Peter came from a well-to-do family. He was the youngest of four children. His father was a banker, and his mother came from an influential family. He did well at school and became a minister as it was secure employment and gave him respect and an air of honesty.

He graduated from a prestigious university and took time off to travel over Europe after graduating. It was in Spain where he had met his present wife, Joan. He was impressed by the size of the churches in Europe and the accumulation of assets the churches had made over the years and, in particular, the Vatican. Joan and Peter toured for a year together, living in backpacker hostels and cheap hotels, before coming home and getting married.

Peter's father had a reputation in the financial industry as being a very hard businessman and would allow nothing to get in his way if he was dealing with an acquisition or merger or taking control of an insolvent client. He was not a religious man and found it hard to see why his son did not follow in his footsteps and become a banker. His other children had all done well and had joined a profession in becoming doctors, lawyers, and bankers – but not Peter. Peter's mother came from an influential family, said to be involved with the Italian Mafia and to have political connections within the senate and judiciary.

Through his father's contacts, Peter was able to get a ministerial job at St Andrew's Church. He had been a minister there for four years. He was ambitious and viewed the church as a business. *If you give your patrons what they want to hear, they will make more donations, and the church will get richer and become more prosperous. To have a poor church does not follow modern thinking and helps no one.* His attitude was that man was put on the earth to develop the world and live a righteous life according to the laws.

Peter's wife, Joan, was also an ambitious woman and was involved in several community programs and bodies and entertained a lot of women's groups at her home to ensure the ladies' vote, according to her thinking.

Peter had the support of the board of elders and the church and prospered immensely since he had begun there as a minister. His father also supported the church, and since Peter had become a minister, attended church regularly. The elders realized that he was not preaching strictly according to the Word of God but didn't care as he was bringing in the money and had all the other ministers on his side except Simon.

The church had moved from a poor establishment with crumbling buildings with limited room to a new church with modern facilities, which was impressive by anyone's standard. All the ministers were paid well and were secure in that they were paid on time and above average wages and enjoyed where they were working as compared to some years ago, when they were not as well off.

Peter realized that the only minister who would not fall in line was Simon and had tried to persuade him to do so for his family's sake as he would not get the benefits elsewhere and as his employment was conditional upon him toeing the line and adopting the modern approach to religion and ministry to ensure the crowds still came in and the cash flow stayed positive.

Chapter 5

The diocese needed money for its refurbishing and asked its ministers to help where possible. Russel was introduced to the archdeacon of the church and made a substantial donation and entertained the archdeacon.

Russel dreamed that night about the rich man asking Jesus what he must do to get eternal life. The second night, he again had a dream and this time about a rich man and a poor man dying, and one went to heaven. The next night, he dreamed about the prodigal son.

After making substantial money and paying little taxes, Russel believed there was still something missing in his life. He approached his friend Peter Sutherland about his dreams. Sutherland, who was out of town that day, put Russel onto his junior minister, who was Simon Fuller. Simon explained the dreams to Russel.

Simon said, 'There were two individuals, one very rich and influential who could afford anything he wanted. The other had no money and was a beggar living outside the rich man's mansion, existing on the scraps the servants would bring out. Both died, and the beggar, who was a God-fearing man and one of faith, went to heaven and was given the wealth that God had promised him.'

'The other, the rich man, went to hell and, to put it lightly, found it intolerable. He yelled out to the angels in heaven to send down the poor man with a drop of water on his finger. But this was denied. He asked for the poor man to go to his family and tell them about where he was, but again, this was not agreed to as they, like him, knew of what would happen when he died and that he would not listen. Whenever they were told of hell, they thought it was crap. It did not suit their purpose to have a hell and therefore didn't want to know about heaven or hell. They considered themselves in heaven already.'

'The story of the prodigal son is of a wealthy man who had two sons. The younger kept pestering his father to give him his inheritance now, to the point where the father gave him 50 percent of his wealth, and the young son left his father's home to find enjoyment and life. He went to the big city and found some friends to go out with, and they helped him waste his money on entertainment, wine, and women. When there was no money left, he found his friends had disowned him, and he was left on his own.'

'He struggled for a while, getting some basic work as a worker in the fields, and then decided to return to his father as his father's servants were living better than he was. So he made his way home. When he was near to his father's house, his father spotted him coming up the road and immediately ran out to greet him. He placed an expensive coat on him and arranged for a banquet in his honour. The other brother, seeing what had taken place, refused to join in, declaring that his younger brother had spent his fortune and should be treated as a servant, not a son.'

'The moral of the stories is that only those who have faith in God will get eternal life, and even if you depart from God, He will forgive you and will be glad to receive you back as one of His own. The dreams are, in reality, telling you, Russel, that you are the wealthy man and will end up in hell unless you seek forgiveness from Jesus, who would be glad to have you back on His terms as long as you have faith in Him.'

Russel said, 'That is a lot of rubbish as I have helped to fund most of the construction of this church and its facilities and humanitarian programs, and you tell me that doesn't count, that it means nothing, and that I should be prepared to go to hell? I have paid to enter heaven.'

Simon said, 'The path to eternal life is not through your wealth but by believing in Jesus Christ and having faith in Him. This alone is the only way you will have eternal life. Not by your good deeds.'

Russel stood up, stared at Simon in disbelief, and walked out of the room. Simon sat for a minute, wondering what had happened, and then got up and went to his office.

When Peter returned the next day, Russel was waiting in his office. He hadn't got much sleep, thinking about what Simon had told him.

Russel said to Peter, 'You told me that good deeds counted in having eternal life, that all I had to do was help the church build its new facilities, and that I would be assured of God's favor. I had a meeting with Simon yesterday about my dreams, and he told me I have been wasting my money on funding the construction of the new church and that none of these counts when I die. I have also made large donations to the archdeacon for the refurbishment of St Nicholas, and all these millions spent doesn't give me any assurance of eternal life but a guaranteed place in hell.'

Peter said, 'Russel, you're upset and haven't slept. Go home and come and see me tomorrow, and we will speak about your concerns. I will try to have the archdeacon speak to you to ensure what we say comes from the highest level.'

Russel said, 'Ring me tomorrow and tell me what time you want to see me. This is important to me.'

Both men shook hands, and Russel moved to go out and was escorted to the front door of the office by Peter. Peter was furious and stormed into Simon's office while Simon was with his secretary.

He said to her, 'Get out. I want to speak to Simon.'

She stared at him and walked briskly out of the office.

Peter said, 'I have had a very aggressive Russel Brown in my office this morning, who has basically told me he is thinking of discontinuing any further payment to our church as you have told him that his contributions amount to nothing when he dies.'

Simon said, 'No, I explained what his dreams meant and that the only way he was going to ensure eternal life was to believe in Jesus Christ and have faith in Him. He would not achieve this through his money or good deeds.'

'You idiot. Do you know what you have done?'

'Yes. I told him the truth.'

'The truth is in the beholder's eye, and you have just shown how far out of touch you are with modern thinking and the new church. This is now out of my hands, and I will have to report it to the archdeacon as he also relies on Russel's donations to refurbish St Nicholas Church.'

'Report it to whoever you want, but if the money means more to you than the truth and what the Bible teaches, then I will not be a party to it. I will have faith in the Lord.'

'Faith. You're joking. He wouldn't help you. That is all garbage. You will be dismissed for this. You will not get another job in this state after what you have done.'

'The sack for telling the truth.'

'Yes. For telling the truth.'

Peter got up and walked out and went to his office. Peter made a phone call to the archdeacon's office and spoke to his secretary. She said that the archdeacon would be in meetings for an hour and that she would convey the message to him when he came out. About an hour later, Peter got a phone call from the archdeacon.

The archdeacon asked, 'Peter, what seems to be the matter?'

Peter said, 'Simon has told Russel that he will not get eternal life by his good deeds, and Russel is on the verge of terminating any further payment towards the refurbishing of your church.'

'Oh, dear. This puts us in a very awkward position. Is Simon willing to tell Russel that he erred in his interpretation of the Bible and that good deeds do come into the evaluation?'

'No, he is sticking to the NEV interpretation of the Bible and refuses to change his position.'

'Have a word with him. Tell him we value his sincerity and service but that he must see our point of view because it takes money to run a church these days. If he cannot fit in, then we must dismiss him, and if anyone enquires, we must advise them we found his service to be poor and not in accordance with the direction of the church. He has a disabled son, I believe. Point out that he will suffer in that with no money, he cannot pay for his son's medical treatment and medication. I hope he comes around for his sake. It is a cruel world out there when you're on your own with no support or money.'

'I will have a word with him and give him the option.'

Peter and the archdeacon broke up, and Peter went back to work. He made several phone calls and dictated a few letters and then asked his secretary to ask Simon to come in.

About a half hour later, Simon came in and said, 'What's up?'

Peter moved to close the door and said to Simon, 'Take a seat. I have just come from talking to the archdeacon, who wants you to have another meeting with Russel and myself and to tell him you were wrong in what you had told him about deeds not being counted to gain eternal life and that they can be used as a substitute for faith.'

'You know as well as I do what the Bible says about how to gain eternal life. All the deeds on Earth will not give you any right to eternal life if you don't believe in Jesus Christ.'

'It is all depends on your interpretation of the Bible.'

'Yes. No doubt you are referring to the one you wrote as it is the one that is leading you to hell.'

'You are being a fool if you believe what was written some two thousand years ago and think that it still applies today. No one supports you in this view, and those who call themselves Christians of the old tradition are questioning their beliefs as they see what is happening in the world. You are a dying breed which faces extinction and humiliation with little support from the community. Face up to it. No one is here to help you on this earth. We are on our own until we die, and that is it.'

'If you think that, why are you still a minister of the church?'

'You haven't seen too many poor churches, have you? There is money to be made in religion.'

'One of us should leave the ministry. I hold my belief, but you have fallen at the feet of Satan and now worship him as king.'

'How dare you say this to me after all that I have done for you and your family! I can see it isn't worthwhile to try to convince you to change your mind and consider Bill, your disabled son, and his special needs, which you cannot afford if they kicked you out of here.'

'I guess the options before me are to fall into line for the good of the church and my family or lose my job and try to make a living as best as I can. Is that right? I am fired if I don't change my faith, putting me and my family at the mercy of the world. Join the Satan mob in promoting lies for the promises that can't or won't be kept.'

'That's exactly right, and once you leave, we will advise anyone who asks us about you, that we had to dismiss you for being not willing to consider the best interests of the church over your own.'

Simon pondered for a minute and said, 'Into your hands, my Lord, I put my faith and soul. No, Peter, you're wrong about what you are doing, and hell is where you will end up. Consumed by fire. You did not get into the ministry to serve God, but yourself and others who think they can buy their way to heaven will join you there. I will not be party to your new religion. Nor will I bow before Lucifer, as it seems you have. I will do the only thing that guarantees me the truth of eternal life, and that is to have faith in Jesus Christ. That's the way I will go. I will get my things and leave my key on your table when I leave.'

Peter got up and grabbed Simon by the scuff of his shirt and with his face right in Simon's face, said, 'You fool. Think of your child and wife. Without a job and health insurance, your whole family will suffer. You won't be able to make a living in this district. The church is too powerful. People will not want to know you as you have left God's service. You will be out on the street without a roof over your head or enough money to buy food. Think of your family, if not yourself.'

Simon said, 'I am thinking about my family. Do you think that the Creator of the world and mankind will let you get away with what you are doing? You have treated Him as if He doesn't exist, and you know He does. You are using His name in vain for profit. He knows what you are doing and will punish you in His own good time. No, I don't want to be part of this scheme of yours to earn thirty pieces of silver. I would prefer to be hungry and without a home but in His care, for I know I am in excellent hands.' Simon, looking very aggressive, continued, 'Let me go. I have been preaching for a long time about faith. Well, I will have to see what faith I have. I will not join your team of antichrists and have the wrath of the Lord upon me. What you have here is the same as Sodom and Gomorrah, and you will be treated in the same way as they were.'

He pushed Peter away from him and left Peter's office. He went to his own office and phoned his wife, Monique.

Simon said, 'Hi, darling. Some bad news. You were right. They have fired me, as you predicted they would. They gave me the option to be one of them or get out. I have decided to put my faith in the hands of the Lord and trust Him to tell me what He wants me to do. I am leaving now and will be home in half an hour. I love you.'

Chapter 6

On Sunday, Peter was at the pulpit, facing the congregation. He said, 'Wasn't that singing great? The sermon today is on the second commandment, "Love thy neighbor". Well, what does this mean? Does it mean you should give all those next door a kiss and a big hug? Well, you can do that if it makes you feel good. I am not sure what reaction you would get from your neighbours if you tried. Or does it mean you should do your best to have a sexual relationship with your neighbours, irrespective of whether they are male or female?'

'No. It means you should respect them and do unto them as you would want them to do unto you. So if you are a sinner and you come to church, you have the same rights as any of us. If you are a homosexual, you may come to church and take part in the community events of the church without being subjected to humiliation or told to leave because of your love for a partner of the same sex.'

'We are not here to judge you, but to bring you into our community. There have been a lot of discussions about same-sex marriages, and the church is trying to distance itself from this. I believe we should encourage same-sex marriages as they will not go away but increase in number as time goes on. It is about time we address the issue and they decide where the church fits into the final decision.'

'We currently have a situation where churches are openly saying we will defy the law and refuse to take part in such marriages, even though it is the law of the land. This is not the Bible speaking. I say, is this not anarchy? And it seems that the church is again trying to re-establish its political connection that was severed in the 1500s. You should not talk behind one's back about a person nor enter into gossip about that person. People in glass houses shouldn't throw stones, as the Bible teaches us.'

'We, as the church, should progress with society and not try to fall back to the BC period or early first century. We live a different life now from how they lived in the past. We have innovations that impact on our daily lives, such as computers, iPhones, and iPads, and live with different customs and laws from those that existed at the time of Jesus Christ. Our laws force us to be more tolerant as we get more immigrants in from different countries.'

'Who is to say that Christianity is the only religion that must be followed when the majority in the world follows different religions? We are not able, under our laws, to discriminate against a race or a religion, and what is to say that our religion is better than another?'

'We should strive to help the needy by ensuring we do not waste what is given to us, but invest our time and money wisely to ensure we can help the Lord do His good work amongst His community. Remember, we all will die someday, and when this happens, we will be judged as to what we have done with our lives in this world.'

'Remember the parable that Jesus told about the master who gave money to three servants? Ten to one, five to the other, and three to the third. Both the first and second servants came back to the master after some time and showed what they had achieved as a profit with the money. The third servant said he didn't want to lose any money, so he buried it and now gave it back. The master was pleased with the first two servants and rewarded them for their ingenuity, while he had the third flogged for wasting the opportunity to gain profits. So, are you going to be flogged or praised?'

'Now, getting back to your neighbor, the real meaning is to go out of your way to help your neighbor, even if it causes you detriment or some inconvenience. If your neighbor rewards you for your kindness, then that is to your benefit. If he doesn't, well, nothing is lost. You have at least tried and will know better the next time.'

'With the world becoming a smaller place and more people traveling, it becomes obvious that there are wealthy people and poor people in this world. Does this mean you have to sell everything you have and give it to the poor? If this was the intention, then I ask you, why hasn't the Catholic Church sold all their vast assets and eradicated poverty? They have the pope, and he doesn't advocate this. What they are saying with their wealth is that you who have little should love your neighbor, but those who have plenty shouldn't worry about helping the poor.'

'How often have you heard about the person, seeing a blind man or a disabled person at the pedestrian lights, taking that person by the hand across the street, and once there, cops abuse, and is smacked with the person's cane and yelled at, "Who do you think you are? Do you think I am a chicken wanting to cross the road? Get me back to where I was standing"? How often have you heard on the news about an innocent bystander going to the aid of a person who is being attacked, only to have been killed by a knife or shot for their good deeds?'

'So where do we stand on this commandment? Well, my belief is that you should have an intention or obligation to help when and where you can but consider at the time, "Is this neighbor ever going to go out of their way to help me?" Your decision surely would, these days, be made on this basis rather than rushing in and putting yourself at risk when your neighbor would not even show appreciation for what you have done or intended to do for them. The world has changed since the first century, and life now is riskier. The number of times you hear of a person being charged with attempted rape or robbery when all they did was stop to lend help seems to be a daily occurrence.'

'Love thy neighbor' is a commandment that, in most cases these days, is not followed for the reasons I have outlined. It is good to know. A nice principle but rarely followed these days. What should you do? Well, that is now up to you to decide.'

The service ended, and the front doors of the church were opened, and the parishioners moved out of the church in an orderly manner. One elderly couple stood near the teacups and discussed the sermon.

One of them said, 'That was an unusual sermon, wasn't it? So I can get to heaven by doing good things? Isn't that what Peter said? Nothing about God or faith? Very unusual.'

'Yes,' said the other, 'and you can tell your neighbor to bugger off when he comes to ask for help. Christianity certainly has changed.'

They moved away from the church to their car, got in, and drove off.

Chapter 7

Northside Chapel and it just turned eleven thirty. All the praises and gratitude had been said. The choir finished singing 'Green Pastures of Home' and moved to their seats.

Peter stood at the pulpit and said, 'We will now conclude the service and allow the family to lay Russel to rest.' Peter leaned into the microphone. 'Russel will be missed, and as we have said, the good will find rest with the Lord. As we have heard from Russel's family and friends, he tried to ensure that he was a benefactor, a supporter of the needy, a contributor to the community, and a recognized supporter of our church. We have seen and noted many times in the newspapers his endless support of causes and to the church. I am sure all will agree that he was a good man. As the curtain closes, we ask the Lord to take care of Russel, and may he rest in peace.'

The curtain closed, and the family walked out, followed by the rest of the assembly.

Ray Brant, a reporter, said, 'In reflection, here is a man who cheated and robbed during his lifetime, and because he gave donations to the church, they descried him as a good man. How often have we heard this? And it is becoming more the case as time goes on, and the influence of the Bible decreases.'

I stood and waited as people moved out of the chapel and thought, *Does Peter really think Russel is with the Lord, or is he willing to say anything that pleases the influential and Russel's family and not God?*

Russel's reputation was known by most, and to stand before a crowd of people and declare this was a saint that we were burying today was more than exaggeration. It was an outright lie. Yet Peter was willing to stand before the assembly and make those statements, which didn't say much about the honesty and integrity of Peter.

I waited for a moment to see what the noise was and, for a minute, thought I could hear a crow crowing, but it was my imagination. *The world has changed, and so has the church. It has lost not only its traditional followers but also its soul and integrity.*

I moved out of the chapel and made my way to my car in the rain. I drove to my office and wrote up my report, which was to be the basis of our story on the front page of our newspaper, with the headlines reading 'Church sends off Saint Russel in an elaborate ceremony'.

I had second thoughts about those headlines whether I should tell the truth, but decided my job was more important to me than the truth. *Who these days believes in the truth, and really, where does it get you?*

Chapter 8

The archdeacon called a meeting of all ministers from his churches in the diocese. Peter was there, but they did not invite Simon.

The archdeacon said, 'We have a problem in the church. An image problem in that we seem to be intentionally excluding or marginalizing some section of the community. It seems that the church is deciding who can attend rather than God, and this puts us in a position where people are turning their backs on us rather than joining our churches. There is a perception that the church is not for sinners but rather for the rich.'

'The church should be a church for all individuals, irrespective of their sins or status in the community. It is necessary that this message gets out into the community with the slogan "God loves us all and especially sinners". They should encourage homosexuals to attend church, and I would leave it up to the individual minister to decide whether he will perform a marriage ceremony if requested to do so. However, if the person is one of influence or political standing, then he should be referred to me before the minister rejects the request if he has done so.'

The archdeacon followed up his presentation to the meeting by writing to each of his ministers, declaring they should tone down their sermons regards homosexuality and justification by faith alone and concentrate on the day of reckoning what they were going to say to Jesus when they stood before Him and explain what they had done with the life He had given them. He urged them to ignore justification by faith or mention Martin Luther, as this was too complicated to be understood by most parishioners who didn't read the Bible and, in reality, would not understand it if they did. He declared the church should be for the people and should cater to their needs in a modern world.

The archdeacon put his papers away after sending out his emails and unlocked a draw in his desk. From there, he took out a laptop computer and switched it on and clicked on a file named Saints. The file opened, and it contains folders of pictures he had taken of children with their vital parts exposed.

He remembered he was looking after his nephew and niece when his sister went shopping. While she was away, he took the children, who were aged three and five, to the toilet and took pictures of them naked. If they said anything, he would simply say he took them to do a wee.

He uploaded the pictures onto his computer and took pleasure in seeing the children naked. He filed them in a file under a separate name and then entered the black web. There, he listed he had pictures for sale, and immediately, there were offers. Payment was made through PayPal and the pictures emailed to the purchasers.

After an hour, the archdeacon shut his laptop down and placed it in his draw and locked the draw. He got up from his desk and noted the time and hurried to his next appointment.

Chapter 9

It was Sunday, and Peter Sutherland stood before the congregation at the pulpit. He hesitated for a few seconds and then said, 'The archdeacon has asked us all to be more tolerant of those who are in minority groups, such as homosexuals, the disabled, and the poor. The groups which historically have not been welcomed in this church.'

'Not that long ago, I saw an alcoholic come into this church and sit down in one of the pews. I noticed some of you moved away from him, but no one went up to him and said, "Can we help you?" No, I don't mean give him a bottle or two or have a drink with him while the sermon is being delivered. I can read your minds, you know. My sermons are not that hard to take. Nor do I mean give him some money so he can race off to the bottle shop. I mean, talk to him and see if he has shelter, food, and fresh clothing. What's his health like? Can we help?'

'It is the same with homosexuals. We do not welcome them at this church. Why? Because they are different, as are the disabled and the poor. We judge this group of people differently. Why? Well, because of what the Bible says, especially the Old Testament. We have to consider that most of the population of our country has voted to allow them to marry and have the same rights that all married couples have.'

'There is a conflict in the Bible regarding homosexuality. On the one hand, the Bible forbids the act, but not the relationship. A man can live with another man and a woman can live with another woman. It is the homosexual act that it forbids. It also says, "Love thy neighbor" and that we should encourage people to become part of our congregation. Yet with this in mind, many have been turned away because of the homosexuality rather than being invited into God's church and encouraged to follow God's Word.'

'I spoke the other day to a mother whose husband died from a heart attack, leaving her on her own to feed, educate, and bring up three children, the eldest being 6 years of age. I commented on the fact that we had not seen her at church for a while and asked what had happened. Had she stopped having faith, or had something cropped up? She advised me that money was scarce in her household, and the children came first, which meant she couldn't afford to spend money on herself and wear the clothes and make-up that other people wore to church. She was questioned some weeks ago by one of our sisters at church and advised, "Surely, you have something better to wear to church than that. This is a place of worship, you know, not the local pub." It is comments like this or insensitivity that show that we have a lot of Pharisees in our church.'

'Last week, I was on a train and spoke to a girl who was sitting near the window. No, you have the wrong idea. I didn't give her a wink and smile. She saw I had a book that I was reading called *Apostles' Creed* and recognized that it was the one she just had finished reading herself. We talked, and I found out that she went to church for many years, but recently, she had stayed away as she was getting people saying to her she should find a young man and settle down. She said she had tried but could find no one she would be comfortable with. I said in jest whether she had thought of an arranged marriage. She had, but then if there was anything like you see in India and other places, she was not willing to chance it. She was basically driven out of the church because some people think they know best and will not let individuals trust God to find them a partner.

'The Bible covers the story of the good Samaritan. You know of it, so I will not go into it in depth. But what I will say is that more and more of us are basically saying to others, "I have the answer to the problems of the world. I know what it would take to fix all these problems – a machine gun, grenades, bombs." You know, Hitler and Stalin used these weapons to eradicate the population, and after killing millions of people, the same minorities still exist. In reality, the answer is love, tolerance, and compassion. We are not asking you to put yourself in their shoes, but allow them the right to exist and find God their own way, not your way.

'This church is for everyone who seeks God, and if you don't like the person's appearance, then take off your shirt and offer it to them. We are told to be disciples of Christ. To become one, you only have to walk down your street and see the problems the community faces. You can lend a hand. You don't have to go overseas or to another country. The problem is right in your own backyard. If those less fortunate than you come to seek God, then help them find Him, and you, too, will be rewarded in heaven. Remember, it is up to God to make the judgement and not you. You are asked to only love your neighbor. Not dictate your beliefs to them.'

Chapter 10

Simon, walking to his house, is confronted by the landlord, who says, 'Simon, you are two weeks behind in your rent, and I have to collect the rent money now, or I am forced to give you an eviction notice, which will mean you have to be out by next Friday.'

Simon said, 'I know we are behind on the rent, but we will get the money to you as soon as I get a job.'

'I heard the church booted you out because you refused to follow orders and were too radical in your thinking for them and refused to change your ways.'

'No, that's not the case. They wouldn't listen when I tried to preach the Word of God. I had a choice to follow the Bible or preach heresy. I chose the Bible and, because of that, lost my job.'

'Well, I don't believe in any of that rubbish and don't care what your problem is. All I want is the rent money, or else you have to be out of here by Friday. Understood?'

'Understood.'

Simon walked home and went into the kitchen, where his wife, Monique, was at the kitchen table.

She looked up and said, 'No luck, I see.'

Simon said, 'No. I have just about been to all the churches in the district, and none will give me a job. They heard what had happened and refuse to employ me as they are most probably doing the same as what Peter is doing preaching to ensure maximum donations and not the true Word of God. It seems no one wants the truth, and as long as their congregation hears what they want to hear, they will continue paying. I am considered a problem, a redneck, who no one wants to have working for them.'

Monique said, 'What are we going to do? We have no money for food. We owe two weeks' rent. Don't have any money for gasoline for the car. Can't buy medicine for Bill and can't afford the bus fare for you to go to an interview. Don't even have any money to buy food for this evening's dinner. We are in a big mess and cannot get out of it.' Monique showed it was getting to her and burst into tears.

Simon said, 'I know it is very bleak for us, and I am also wondering from where the next meal is going to come from. We can only pray and ask the Lord for His help.'

Monique said, 'Pray? That will not get us anywhere. That's all I have been doing, but there is no one there. The Lord isn't hearing our prayers. I am praying to no one. There is no response, as if the Lord has abandoned us, and what Peter Sutherland said is right. He will not be punished for his actions, but we will be for ours. Is the devil stronger than God and has he stopped God from doing the right thing? Peter is certainly doing well, and we say he's wrong, and we are bankrupt and say we are right. I pray, and it is as if the Lord has gone on holiday to Pluto and has told the angels not to bother Him with our problems.'

'Yes, I concede that is the case, but even when it appears they have abandoned us in the wilderness, we should still maintain our faith and know that He will help us. We must have faith.'

'Simon, we cannot be in a worse situation than we are in currently.'

'Unfortunately, you are wrong. I met the landlord, who was waiting outside of our house. He said unless we pay the rent by Friday, he wants us out of the place.'

Monique burst into tears again and ran from the kitchen. Simon sat and bowed his head and prayed.

'Lord, I know you are there, and thank you for the time you have given me to contemplate my faith and to draw a conclusion, whether I believe in you. I do, and while I don't understand why this is happening to us, I know you will help us as all things are possible unto you. Lord, we are in a crisis, with no money, no work, and no food for the baby. Our telephone has been cut off for non-payment of our bill, and we now have been told to pay the rent, or they will evict us. Please. We desperately need your intervention and help. In Jesus's name, I ask. Amen.'

Simon moved to get up from the kitchen table when there was a knock at the front door. He thought, *Not another bill collector.* He moved to the door and cautiously opened it. There was a man standing there with a woman.

Simon said, 'Can I help you? Are you broken down, lost?'

The stranger replied, 'No. I hope we are not intruding. My name is John Phillips, and this is my wife, Alice. We used to go to your former church and have heard that they fired you because you would not preach the lies that they were. We have left that church because they are not preaching the Bible and basically make up their rules as they go along. They do not have room for Christ and refuse to preach about the cross. We have been going around to various churches in the district, but they all seem to do the same thing. Can you tell us where you are setting up so we can join your church and tell others who feel the same way?'

'Thank you, but at present, I cannot get a job as a minister and have been out of work for the last two weeks.'

'How are you managing with food and other necessities?'

'We are finding it tough but are managing. It is a struggle, but I am sure with the good Lord's help, we'll make it.'

Monique came out of the bedroom and stood at the front door and said, 'Managing? You are kidding. We don't have any food. We cannot buy medicine for our baby, and we are going to be kicked out of our house because we are behind in the rent.'

Simon said, 'Monique, we shouldn't burden these good people with our problems. I am sure they have enough of their own. I am sorry. My wife is stressed out and finds it hard to accept that we are in somewhat of a difficult situation without what seems any way out of it.'

John said, 'We are asking you to form a church so those who want the true Word of the Lord can come and receive it. There are others like us who are also willing to help form this church. Will you be our minister?'

'John, I appreciate you want to have an evangelical church established here, but we most probably won't be around for much longer. As Monique has mentioned, things are not looking too good for us, and they most probably will get worse before they get better.'

'Let me get this right. Your problem is money, not faith, or is it both? How much money must I give you for you to guarantee that I will have the blessing of the Lord, forgiveness of my sins, and eternal life?'

'I could not accept a cent from you, for Jesus Christ died for you, so your sins were forgiven, and if you believe in Him, you will have eternal life.'

'Then how much money would I have to give you to receive Jesus's blessing?'

'Again, John, His blessing is never bought. It is given freely to those who believe in Him and request it.'

'Then what would it take to keep you here and establish an evangelical church here? I understand that you have been out of work for a couple of weeks and that things are getting hard, but I am prepared to pay you five thousand dollars to stay and establish a church here in this town and not run away from these crooks who are preaching modernity and not the Word of the Lord.'

Simon, not really knowing what to say, paused and said, 'We appreciate your gesture, John, but it would not be right for us to accept your money. We cannot buy Christ.'

John said, 'You unfortunately misunderstand. I am not buying Christ, but trying to help His church. You can take the money on the condition we have a minister, and you will look after our congregation as best as the good Lord allows.'

Monique said, 'Simon, take it as it's God's answer to our prayers.'

Simon said, 'It is against my character to accept this type of money, but I would like to establish a church and ensure the Word of the Lord is heard instead of the lies spoken by Peter Sutherland and others.'

John said, 'Good.' John took out the pouch from his pocket and handed it to Simon. 'We have a deal.'

Simon put out his hand and said, 'We have a deal, or is it a covenant with the Lord? How do I get in contact with you about venues and other matters?'

John said, 'My contact details are on the note that I left in the pouch.'

Simon opened the pouch and saw the note and said, 'You are the vice president of the local bank.'

John said, 'That, I am, and I can afford to assist the Lord. However, that's not why I am here. When I was in my early teen years, I was a street kid. I never knew my mother or father. They fostered me out from about 5 years of age and found myself in most cases with families who used me for pornography or their own sexual pleasures. I ran away from these homes and eventually found myself on the streets with no money or help. I had to raid garbage tins to find food and clothing. Sometimes the women in the houses would come out with food or clothing and give it to me or leave it out for kids like me.'

'One night I had a dream which told me to go to the local railway station, and there on the street, I would find a small pouch which would contain five thousand dollars. I was to take this money and find myself a place to sleep and find a job. The dream ended with the words "The Lord needs you. Follow His commands and be blessed". I went to the railway station and could only see many people walking to the station and then going down the stairs to get on their train, while others were coming out of the station. I looked around and couldn't see any pouch and eventually was ready to give up. I sat down on a bench, thinking what this was all about, when suddenly, a pouch came flying along the ground, as if someone had kicked it out of their way. It landed right at my feet. I picked it up, and sure enough, there was money in it, and later, when I counted it, there was five thousand dollars.

'I used the money to find a cheap room to stay in and went and got some clothes at the local charity op shop. On my way back to my room, I passed a large factory which had a sign showing "General Hand Required". I walked in there, and they took me on. Over the years, through hard work, I received promotions and could go to night school, where I learned to read and write at 25. I continued school and graduated from high school and then went on to university, where I got my degree in finance and law. With this, I could get a job with a stockbroking firm and could make some money in dealing in shares. I got married and had a family. I then got a job with a large bank and, over the years, was able to work my way up to vice president of retail banking.

'In 2000, I warned the bank regarding their practices towards securitization, but they wouldn't listen. Their practices were verging on criminality. I was a voice in the wilderness, not willing to be a party to their dishonesty. They basically forced me to resign, and of course, no one would believe me when I told them of the practices and forewarned them of the disaster that would happen if it continued and so left them and joined the local bank, which has ethical practices. In 2008, my former bank was forced to go into liquidation as they had so mismanaged the bank that it could not be rescued and collapsed. A lot of investors ended up losing a lot of their savings because of the dishonesty and greed of a few executives.'

'I never have forgotten what the Lord did for me when I was on the street amongst the drug addicts and homeless and since then have given out several pouches to people in need in the Lord's name. In your case, I was part of the congregation that has seen what is going on in your previous church. It is the same greed that affected my former bank, and it only leads to destruction.'

'Last week, I had a dream which showed me sitting on the same bench when I couldn't find the pouch of money at the railway station when I was a teenager. Suddenly, a pouch came sliding along the ground and stopped at my feet. I was looking at it when a man appeared in front of me, saying, "John, take the pouch and give it to Simon" at an address which he gave me, with the instruction "Simon is to establish a church where the teaching shall be under my Word". I have received this vision several times, and except for the first time, the same man has appeared. He dresses differently and is always gentle in manner and friendly. But I can never remember what he looks like. I would recognize him if I met him in the street but cannot describe his features, except his clothes were the same as you and I would wear. As soon as you opened the door, I knew we were at the right address.'

Simon asked, 'Where are we to establish the church?'

John said, 'I know the council has a hall we can use for Sunday services, which will not cost us anything, as it is for community purposes. I will arrange for it to be available to us every Sunday. I know the major, who will always be willing to do me a favor.'

'Great. Let's spread the word and establish our church.'

'We will be in touch.'

'Thanks for being the messenger.'

The men shook hands, and the ladies kissed, and John and Alice left. Simon and Monique sat down in the lounge and looked at each other, and wondered about what had happened.

Both joined hands, and Simon said, 'Our Father, we thank you for the miracle you have given us in answer to our prayers. May we never lose our faith or have doubt in you. May the Lord direct us how this money is to be spent and help us establish your church. Thank you, Father. In Jesus's name, amen.'

Chapter 11

Simon said before the congregation, 'This being our first church meeting together, I believe it necessary to touch on the point of what is a church. We have decided that we do not agree with – nor are we willing to follow – the teachings of the other churches in the dioceses for one reason or another, but mainly because of their teachings.'

'So what is our church going to be that the others are not? First, before we answer that question, we must find out what a church is. Is it where we meet every Sunday? Well, we can do that at the local pizza shop. Is it where we meet to discuss Christ or biblical issues? Well, we can do that in a hall like this one.'

'The church is what God created to be a place where those who believe can meet and pray together, where the congregation can assemble and discuss religious issues, and where we can help one another to overcome adversities and support one another. God said, "Where two or more are gathered in my name, I shall be there." So the church is just that. Us gathering in God's name to worship Him, knowing He is present amongst us.'

'Many of us have problems and are reluctant to discuss them with our family or friends for fear that we will tag them as nutcases or troublemakers. Life is hard these days, and there are a lot of stormy clouds through which you have to travel. Jesus established the church for the purpose that we can help one another through times of difficulty and to spread His word.'

'In the days of the fifteenth century, politics and religion were entwined, and fear of God's wrath was always part of what they taught to the people. When politics was separated from religion, there was nothing that was there to fill the gap. Religion has since tried to fall back on the Baptist's cry of "Repent, for the day of reckoning will shortly come!" They did not adopt a new way of teaching the Bible, but tried to use the old brimstone and fire approach to get people to accept Christ.'

'They did not teach most of the population why they are on Earth, and since they have a choice, they have decided they did not want to know or have anything to do with religion. The movement now is towards looking after the self at all costs, not the community, the church, or your neighbor. This, coupled with populism and the increasing technical innovations throughout the world, has encouraged the young "to be your own master, and your destiny is in your hands". The population has, in fact, fallen for this rot.'

'The church now finds itself with an aging congregation and fewer younger patrons to take their place. The parents and the church have not taught the younger generation the facts about why they have been placed on this earth and their linkage to the sacrifice God has made to ensure they have eternal life.'

'The Bible is as relevant today as it was in Jesus's day, and the message is still applicable today as it was then. It is when people change their God and "the teachings" that we have chaos as each person reckons their God is better than anyone else's, but they are comparing themselves with others. Why does the church find itself in such a confrontational situation? It is because so many blame the church for lack of spiritual support and help when they need it. In short, the church has let them down in these areas.'

'The other reason is because the church has tried to be non-political when it comes to issues that affect its congregation. It has left its congregation to take up issues rather than the church doing it. It has taken a holier-than-thou approach on issues and therefore does not speak for the community. The numbers in the church should be enough to persuade politicians to sit up and listen and not to trounce our faith, but not a word is spoken by the church on behalf of its congregation. Until it is too late.'

'God is part of your everyday life, and so should the church. We are not a trade union where fees are demanded annually, but we should not put up with the erosion of Christian faith, which is progressing through our parliaments by minorities, who glorify their achievements with little opposition.'

'In many countries throughout the world and in some of our own states, you cannot have a Christian class during school hours. Christianity is not taught in schools anymore. In its place is a subject called ethics. The purpose of life, why you are born – such topics are not taught anymore in schools, and no one cares about it.'

'The next generation being born will not know the purpose of their birth, and this is intentional. They will not know that they must ask for God's help to get eternal life. They will be born in sin and bow before Lucifer and declare him king and not be told the truth about what is going to happen to them when they die.'

'What is the church doing for them? Nothing, as the majority, is only interested in the money that can be gained from religion and does not spread the message according to the Bible. "Save souls? Bring people to God? Well, that's too hard. We might just go along with the flow and make a living out of religion and not worry about our Lord or our fellow man."

'It is Christ who wants us to be people who take religion seriously. Jesus has said religion is a full-time occupation, and your daytime job is secondary to it and not the other way around. Most people don't want others to know that they are Christians except on Sundays, at meetings like this. If asked, they mumble something that leaves the listener unsure. The simple "Yes" is rarely given or "Yes, I go to church".

'When confronted with a statement or a fact that is contrary to the Christian belief, the Christian bends at the knee and declares Lucifer king as he doesn't want to be the odd one out or oppose his colleagues. They threw his faith through the window, and the way of the world takes control. Most Christians think they can have a foot in both camps. As soon as Sunday comes along, they ask the Lord to forgive them of their sins, and they think they are back to where they were before they had sold out. Unfortunately, that is not the case, and the church has done little to educate its congregation that this is not possible. You cannot hold dual citizenship when it comes to belief in God. You either believe in the Lord and have faith, or you are an outsider taking up a pew.'

'The church does not hammer this home enough, and basically, out of a thousand worshippers, there would be a dozen who will be true believers. This is the problem the church faces and why, most times, the church is ineffective in trying to combat issues affecting its congregation. Unfortunately, the congregation is neutral and does not support the church by faith and action. Christ asked you to become a disciple and spread the Word.'

'Let's begin to stand up for Jesus Christ, our Lord. I remember seeing pictures of our country back in the thirties and forties. One thing that struck me was the number of houses that had a cross or a plaque attached to the front of the house. Most read, "Christ is Lord." Some had a cross attached to the plaque, while others had things like "The Lord's Home" or other slogans which recognized their belief in Jesus Christ. I must say the one that has always stayed with me is "Home Sweet Home, the House of Our Lord". You don't see that these days. In fact, most people prefer to keep the fact that they are Christians a secret.'

'Well, I am telling you that a hurricane is coming soon, and for those people who have a cross outside their front door or a plaque recognizing them to be of the faith, their homes will be spared. For those who do not take this warning seriously, you can take the risk and the consequence. Let's see how many of you stand up and agree to outwardly show off your faith as being a Christian rather than being closet Christians. So we have much to do with our church in getting it recognized on the Web and established to confront the issues necessary to defend our faith.'

'Let's bow our heads and pray. Father, we are assembled in your name and ask that you bless each one of us. Give us strength to have faith in you and stand up for our faith when the opportunity arises. May we be your disciples and spread the word as you command? We ask in your holy name. May our church prosper in spreading your word. Amen.'

The congregation stood up and started to walk out of the hall.

Chapter 12

Without a job and little money, Simon sought a job outside of the ministry. Simon thought, *It was good enough for Paul to go back to his trade in repairing tents, so why shouldn't I look for something other than ministry which will pay the bills and feed the family?*

Simon found a position in a large warehouse and was trained to pick orders and load trucks and become a forklift driver. His wife stayed home and looked after their disabled son and their teenager, who was still at school.

At morning break and lunchtime, the men and women at the warehouse congregated and talked amongst themselves.

After a busy session in the morning, the men and women were in the lunchroom when Simon said to one man, 'Sam, what's up? You seem to look as if the world was on your shoulders.'

Sam looked up and said, 'It is private.'

His mate Ron said, 'Private, my ass. We all know that you and your missus are having a hard time and most probably will separate and divorce.'

Sam said, 'Yes. I can't see a way out of our problem. We have just drifted apart and do not seem to have any time for each other. It will be the kids who will suffer when we split up. I don't know whether I will get to see them once we divorce.'

Simon asked, 'Sam, are you a religious man?'

Sam replied, 'I went to church, and we went to see the minister there at St Andrews, Peter Sutherland, but he said, "see a counselor and seek out your own problems."'

Simon looked at Sam and said, 'That's no help. Why don't you and your missus come to my house tonight and have dinner with me and my wife so we can discuss your problem? I may have an answer for you.'

Sam said, 'We will try anything, but I don't believe anything will help us, but I will try.' Sam phoned his wife and told her what had happened, and she agreed to go to Simon's place for dinner.

Simon telephoned Monique. 'Hi, love. I need your help. One of my workmates is having a marital problem, and I would like to help. If it is OK with you, I have invited them to dinner tonight so I can discuss it with them.'

Monique got angry and said, 'Are you joking? I haven't got anything I can prepare for them and on such short notice.'

Simon smiled and said, 'Surely, you have two fish and a couple of bread rolls.'

Monique said, 'hilarious. That is about all we have. If you want them here, then it will be all right. I will say a prayer and see what comes of it.'

Simon got back to work and clocked off at the end of his shift and went home. Monique had already cooked a meal and had fed the kids, who were in their bedrooms, watching TV, and soon after, Sam and his wife arrived. The introductions were made, and each of the couples sat down to talk. Sam explained that they each still loved each other, but something was not right with their lives. Something was missing, and he could not explain what.

Sam's wife, Mary, piped up and said, 'We were happy when we had the kids, but the last year or so, we have stopped going to functions, to church, and seeing our friends.'

Simon, after listening for a while, said, 'I think your problem lies in that you have been part of a close-knit community which, over time, has drifted apart. Also, by the sound of it, you were always going to church and taking part in the programs that were held there. But since your former minister left, the new minister seems to concentrate on worldly matters and not on the Word of God. I would like to propose a solution which will need both of you to do something on an ongoing basis for seven days. Do you agree?'

Both said, 'Yes. What are you proposing?'

Simon said, 'For the next seven days, you are to stop what you are doing and say to yourself, "Is this what Jesus would do before proceeding?" If it is not, stop and think what Jesus would do and then do it.'

Sam said, 'I don't know.'

Mary said, 'It is worth a try.'

Sam said, 'All right. I am prepared to give it a go since you are. How did you think of this solution? Are you a religious person?'

Simon said, 'Yes, a disciple of Christ.'

Sam said, 'Ah.'

They then moved to the dining room and had dinner afterwards. They broke up, and Sam and Mary went home.

Chapter 13

Sam got up on Saturday morning and, after making himself breakfast, cut the grass.

He came in after finishing, and Mary was up and said, 'I have to go shopping this morning as we are out of a lot of things.'

Sam said, 'I will give you the money, and you take the car and go yourself.' He then stopped and pondered for a few seconds and said, 'On second thought, I will go with you as there will be a lot of heavy bags to carry.'

Mary said, 'Thanks. I was hoping you would say that.'

They drove to the shopping centre, and Sam parked the car. They got out and went into the centre. Sam got a shopping trolley and they moved down the aisle. Mary got some milk and put it into the trolley, and they moved to the meat department.

She started looking at the chops, and Sam said, 'We can't afford chops. Get some patties or sausages.'

Mary put the chops back and got some sausages, and they moved on. They came to the cereal aisle, and Mary grabbed a packet of cornflakes.

Sam said, 'No, we don't want that. Take the other packet. It's cheaper.'

Mary looked at Sam and said, 'Look, you won't eat that rubbish. You will take one mouthful and spit it out and throw the rest in the garbage bin.'

Mary put the Cornflakes in the trolley, and Sam got angry. His expression was as if he was going to explode.

Mary said, 'Look, Sam, why don't you sit down and wait for me outside the supermarket? I'll finish the shopping, and we can get a cup of coffee.'

Sam said, 'What? Spend money on coffee? You're joking.'

Sam threw the trolley at Mary and went off in a huff. Mary got her composure and continued her shopping. She went through the checkout and pushed the trolley to where Sam was waiting.

Sam asked, 'How much did that cost?'

Mary replied, 'The usual – 260 dollars.'

'We will go broke, the way we spend money.'

'We have to eat. You will be the first to complain if something is tasteless or different.'

Sam gave an 'Ahhh!' and took the trolley.

Mary asked Sam, 'Are we going for a cup of coffee?'

Sam replied, 'No, it is cheaper at home. They charge you three dollars for hot water. No. I can do better at home and save a quid.'

They did their shopping and came home. Sam went to the TV and switched it on and sat down. Mary unpacked. Sam got up and gave her a hand and then went back to the TV and switched on the football game.

Mary asked, 'Sam, can you take out the garbage?'

Sam replied, 'Surely, you can do that. All right. Jesus. OK.'

'What? Did you say something?'

'Yes, I was having a conversation with me mate Jesus. I will do it now.'

Sam got up, took the papers and boxes from the shopping, placed them in the recycle bin, went back into the house, and sat in front of the TV.

After about a minute, Mary yelled out to Sam, 'Sam, will you get me the shears? I need to cut the chicken in half!'

Sam replied, 'I will get them. They are in the garage on the back shelf. I left them there last week while I was cleaning them. I'll cut the chicken for you.'

Sam got up, still looking at the TV game being played, and went into the garage. He moved towards the back wall quickly, as he didn't want to miss much of the game being shown on TV. There were shelves there which he had erected, and he had placed some paint cans and other things on so they would be out of the way and off the ground.

He reached for the shears and put his foot on a marble, which one kid had dropped. His body went forwards, straight into the shelving on the back wall. He tried to grab onto something to stop himself from falling and grabbed one upright, which caused the shelves to collapse and tins of paint to fall on him. One large can of paint from the top shelf fell onto the shelf below. The top lid flew off, and the can hit Sam on the head, spilling the paint over him. Sam was knocked unconscious, and the top and second shelf came down with a great crash, which could be heard in the kitchen.

Mary heard the crash and ran to the garage to find Sam unconscious, bleeding from the head and paint and cans all over the floor. She got to Sam and yelled out, 'Sam! Sam! Speak to me!'

Sam showed no sign of life. Mary rushed into the house with paint on her hands, grabbed the telephone, and called emergency services.

The operator asked, 'What do you require?'

Mary said, 'My husband has had a can of paint fall on him and has been knocked out and is bleeding from a wound to his head.'

'What is your address?'

'It's 666—Ahhh, no, no, 66 Transgression Street.'

'Code one. At address 66 Transgression Street. Man knocked unconscious with hit to the head. Ma'am, we have dispatched an ambulance to your address. They are in your area, so they should be there shortly.'

'I can hear their siren. Thank you.'

Mary went to the front door just as the ambulance pulled into the driveway. Two paramedics stepped out and rushed towards Mary.

The paramedics asked, 'Where is he?'

Mary led them to the garage, where Sam was lying.

The first paramedic leaned over Sam and got a handful of paint. He asked, 'Ma'am, do you have any rags so we can dry up some of this paint?'

The second paramedic took his stethoscope out of his bag and listened to Sam's chest. He put his fingers on his wrist and waited a few seconds. He said, 'We are losing him.'

Mary yelled, 'God, no! No, not my Sam! Please, no! No, don't let this happen!' She became hysterical.

The first paramedic grabbed her and pushed her out of the garage.

The second paramedic yelled out, 'No pulse! Get the defibrillator!'

The man ran to the ambulance and took out some equipment. He opened it quickly and took out two pads and yelled out, 'All clear!' and looked to ensure his mate was not touching Sam. He placed both pads on Sam's chest and pressed a button, which sent a shock into Sam. Mary looked at what was happening. She was still crying and saw Sam shake from the Shockwave.

The first paramedic yelled out, 'Nothing! No pulse! Hit him again!'

The second paramedic dialed up the charge, put the pads on Sam's chest, said, 'Clear!' and hit the button, sending a Shockwave through Sam.

Sam started to breathe but could not speak and fell back with his eyes closed.

The first paramedic grabbed the stethoscope and listened to Sam's chest and said, 'His heart is coming around, but we better get him to the hospital quickly, as he is liable to have another heart attack.'

They grabbed their bags and took them to the ambulance. They then brought back a stretcher and left it outside the garage. They lifted Sam up, carried him to the stretcher, laid him down on it, and wheeled it to the ambulance. They opened the ambulance doors and lifted the stretcher into the ambulance.

Mary said, 'I'm coming with you.'

One paramedic said, 'You better get in as this is going to be under siren and a quick drive.'

Mary got into the ambulance. The other paramedic got in the back and was checking on Sam's heart rate. They drove off.

One paramedic grabbed the two-way radio and said, 'Base, we have a male with severe head injury and cardiac arrest. Inform emergency, we will be at the hospital in ten minutes.' He put the radio into its cradle and said, 'Siren and lights on. Hang on. This is going to be a quick trip.'

The paramedic in the back said, 'He's 160 over 110. You better be prepared to pull over if he gets worse.'

The ambulance sped through the quiet suburban streets onto the freeway with siren blaring. Most drivers moved over, but some didn't care and obstructed the ambulance.

The driving paramedic muttered, 'I bet they would move over if it was one of their relatives.'

They arrived at the hospital, and two nurses rushed to the ambulance, putting an oxygen mask on Sam.

The first nurse asked, 'What's his reading?'

One paramedic said, 'Last was 175/115, with no reaction to light, showing brain damage.'

She looked at Sam and said, 'The head is swelling. We will need to rush him to the operating theatre.'

They all took the stretcher out of the ambulance and rushed Sam down the hospital hall into the operating theatre.

The first nurse asked, 'Where did all this paint come from?'

One paramedic replied, 'From heaven. It fell on him, cracking his head open.'

Mary stumbled out of the ambulance, bewildered by what had happened and thinking the worst – that Sam would die. She got into the hospital and didn't know where to go. If Sam died, she pondered what she should do. She couldn't think that this would happen and burst into tears.

After about a minute, a lady in a pink shirt and slacks came up to her and said, 'Hi. You look like you need a friend. My name's Rachel. I am one of the volunteers at the hospital. What seems to be the problem?'

Mary told Rachel what had happened in between sobs and said, 'The way they were talking, Sam might not make it. I don't know what I will do without him.'

Rachel said, 'Let me take you to the waiting room near the operating theatre so the doctor can speak to you when Sam comes out of the operation.'

They walked down several hallways silently until they reached a waiting room.

Mary was led in, and Rachel said, 'You can stay here until they have completed the operation. Is there anything I can bring you, or would you like to contact members of your family?'

Mary suddenly realized she had left the house unlocked and without her purse and money. She remembered her children were with her mother and were not due back home for another few days. How was she going to get back home? The only name that came to her that would help would be Simon.

Mary asked Rachel if she could use the phone to call a friend, and Rachel handed her the phone on the table in the room. Mary dialed telephone assistance and asked for Simon's number, which was given to her by the operator. She rang Simon, told him what had happened, and asked him to go to her home, lock it up, and bring her handbag to the hospital, the one that was on a table at the entrance.

Simon was concerned about what Mary had told him and told Monique. Simon went to Mary's house, locked the place up, found her handbag, and set off for the hospital. He got to the hospital and asked for directions to the waiting room and finally found Mary there on her own, crying and looking a mess.

Simon asked, 'Any news of him?'

'No. They are telling me nothing, and it has already been two hours.'

'These things take time. We can only do our best and leave the matter in Jesus's hands. Have you sought God's help?'

'Ha! It was the good Lord who did this. "If Sam didn't ask for your help, he would still be in one piece." Now because of the good Lord, he is on his way to the grave.'

'I don't believe this happened because of Jesus. Let us pray and ask for His help and strength.'

Simon sat down near Mary and took her hand and prayed. After his prayer, he sat back in the chair and wondered why this happened to these decent people. It always seemed to be the innocent and most vulnerable who copped it in the neck, and Simon had no answer for it.

He sat back and asked Mary, 'Can I get you a cup of coffee?'

Mary replied, 'That would be good. Thank you.'

Simon went out of the room to find a coffee dispenser.

When he was out of the room, a doctor came in with his operating gown still on and said, 'I believe your name is Mary.'

Mary said, 'That's correct, and who are you?'

'My name is Preston. I was the doctor who operated on your husband. We have had to put him in a coma to allow his brain to adjust. It swelled up, owing to the hit by the paint can.'

'Is he going to be all right?'

'We cannot say, as he had a heart attack when he was unconscious, so we do not know whether we are dealing with a cardiac problem or a brain problem, or both. He is being taken to a room, and once they have transferred him, they will come and get you.'

'Thank you.'

The doctor walked out. After a few minutes, Simon walked in, and Mary told him what the doctor had told her.

Simon gave her the coffee, and Mary sipped it and said, 'Pretty poor coffee. Must have been made from burned sticks.'

They both sat in silence for a minute. Then a nurse appeared and asked them to follow her. She took them both to a room where Sam was lying still with an oxygen mask on and breathing irregularly. Sam had his head bandaged and still had signs of blue paint on his shoulders and upper chest. He was breathing shallowly. Mary moved close to him and took Sam's hand, and Simon grabbed a chair and slid it closer to the bed. Mary sat on the chair, looked at Sam, and cried.

Simon said, 'Mary, God is looking after Sam. Let us say a prayer.'

She nodded, and Simon said a prayer while Mary was holding Sam's hand. Mary looked at Sam, hoping that there was some sign from him showing he was all right and would come back to her, but there was none.

Simon sat in the corner for about half an hour and then said, 'Mary, we have got to go. You need a break from this, and I have to get home to the family.'

Mary replied, 'No, you go. I will stay here.'

'All right, but call me if there is any change or if you want to go home. I will come and pick you up.'

'Thanks, Simon. You have been a loyal friend.'

Simon left and, on his way out, stopped in a lounge and said a prayer for Sam, asking the Lord to watch over him and help him recover. He then left the hospital and drove home.

Mary was still beside Sam's bed, holding his hand, staring at him for some sign of life or for him to recognize her. It was 11:00 p.m., and she dozed off in the chair while holding Sam's hand. A nurse awakened Mary, saying she must give Sam an injection and change his dressing and asking if she would like to go home and get some sleep.

Mary said, 'I am not leaving Sam's side. He is all I have, and I want to be with him should he pass on.'

The nurse said, 'Well, he is not out of danger yet. Why don't you get a cup of coffee and throw some water on your face while I attend to Sam?'

Mary said, 'I think that is a good idea.'

Mary went out and made her way to the bathroom and washed her face. She looked in the mirror and saw how she had aged and wondered what would have happened to her if she had left Sam as planned before the Jesus experiment. She finished washing herself, went and got a cup of coffee, and came back to Sam's room.

The nurse had completed changing Sam's dressing, and a fresh bandage was on his head. Mary moved over to the window, looked out, and wondered what she would do without Sam, whom she now recognised had been always by her side and the only person who always had been her rock. She had already phoned her parents, who were looking after the kids, who had not been told about their father. Mary moved back alongside Sam and sat down beside him.

She took his hand and said a prayer. 'Lord, all things are possible unto you. Please bring my Sam back to me. Amen.'

She sat there for an hour and slipped into a mini sleep. She was awakened by a twitch in Sam's hand but immediately thought this was her imagination and that it was a reaction to the shock she had been through. She noticed that Sam's eyelids were twitching and screamed out for the nurse.

A doctor came running into the room and asked what was wrong. She pointed to Sam, and the doctor noticed the eyelid's movement. He called for Dr. Preston, who came immediately. Preston ordered the discontinuation of the coma-inducing drugs and that Sam be placed on saline to flush all the drugs out of his body. He advised Mary that it could be twenty-four hours before they would get some sign of the extent of Sam's injuries.

Mary stayed alongside Sam and still held his hand. Around three o'clock in the morning, Mary was startled by someone squeezing her hand. She realised it was Sam and said, 'Thank God you are still with me. Lord, thank you for not taking my Sam.'

Sam gently squeezes Mary's hand and tries to say some words.

Mary could not hear what he was saying and said, 'Sam, rest. You can talk later.'

But Sam persisted in trying to say something. Mary got up but was still holding Sam's hand and moved closer to him to hear what he was saying, and she put her ear close to his lips and heard, 'God refused to take me because you prayed for my return.'

Mary smiled and understood that Jesus had allowed this to happen, so they knew the extent of their love for each other and that they had His blessing to live a fruitful life. Mary rang Simon and gave him the good news.

Two days later, Sam was sitting up in bed and could talk to the doctors and recognized his visitors and Mary. One week later, Sam was discharged from hospital and went home with Mary.

Chapter 14

It was Sunday, and Simon got ready to give his sermon for the ten-o'clock mass. The singing finished, and they read a chapter in the Bible from Genesis covering the Creation and Adam. Simon then stepped forward to the pulpit.

Simon said, 'In meeting with you over the last month or so, I can see that there are different opinions regarding some of the basics, which you have asked me to clarify.'

'The first question is, where do we come from? This is an unknown. The Bible doesn't tell us. However, there have been several scholars over the last century and others who have had some opinion on this topic, but unfortunately, there have been no firm conclusions, only hypotheses.'

'From my part, I would prefer to take the lead from the American Negros who used to work on the fields in the Southern United States, who, during their day, used to sing, "Swing low, sweet chariot, coming forth to carry me home." Home – where is that? Heaven! So, according to them, we came from heaven. There have been, over the years, other groups who have drawn the same conclusion, and I agree with them. So let's say we come from heaven.'

'The question that must be asked is if it is so important to know what our purpose is on this earth, why aren't we taught about it in schools and other places, so we know the truth? Most churches don't cover the subject and merely emphasize on the crucifixion and resurrection without starting from the beginning and how we entered the world and the choice we must make from the beginning.'

'The answer is that the church is a poor teacher, and one hour a week is not enough time to cover the subject adequately. This, coupled with the fact that most parents were never taught about this subject, and therefore, they do not cover it with their children, and so they do not pass the knowledge on from one generation to another. This, coupled with the fact that families seldom sit together for a meal, and therefore, the art of conversation has been lost.'

'As time goes on, the parents develop mental problems or addictions and don't seek guidance from Jesus Christ but rather, relief from drugs and alcohol, and their children see this happening and follow the same path, generally from their early years. After many generations have passed, there is an increasing need for Jesus Christ, but no one knows of Him or how to get in contact with Him. Has anyone got His mobile number? Revelations tell us that this problem will not go away but will become a tsunami as time goes on, with the Christian being very much the minority and persecuted.'

'The next question is why? Were we so stupid that we left a comfy position under the protection of God to come to a place like Earth, where there is sin and death? No, we had no choice. You see, when God created the earth, Lucifer was in charge of the earth. At the time of creation, there was a challenge to God's authority by Lucifer. There was evil in Lucifer, and one third of the heavenly population supported him in his plan to overthrow the establishment in heaven and take control.

It sounds a bit like what we see in parliaments or congress these days throughout the world.'

'God knew of what was going to happen and decided to concentrate all evil that existed in the universe in one place – namely, Earth. So Lucifer and his millions of supporters were tossed out of heaven and established themselves on Earth. Lucifer rules the earth and, over the years, has increased his army of followers by ensuring the inhabitants of the world don't follow the Word of God but rather follow him.'

'Adam was created and placed in Eden and was, at the time of creation, as pure and innocent as God. He was made in the image of God. He knew nothing of what had transpired and of God's plan. He went about his business, and when Eve was created, the devil had to do something to ensure the world was not populated by humans who believed in and supported God. He had to make sure that man was not born in righteousness, but in sin. You know what happened. Eve ate of the fruit, and sin entered both of them. From that moment, all those born on this earth were born in sin and not in righteousness. Did the devil outsmart God? No, for God knew what the devil was up to and used his treachery for His own purposes.'

'God decided it was not enough to create life in an environment of innocence, purity, and truth. It had to be earned rather than gifted. Otherwise, it would not be appreciated. He had previously given this to the angels in heaven freely, and one third of His creation turned against Him and followed evil, a sinful life. The fact that His creation had the right of choice meant that evil was a possibility which He had to contend with, especially with His newest creation, man.'

'God decided to allow all the souls in heaven to be progressively sent to Earth so their faith could be tested and to give them the freedom of choice, good or evil. If they decided not to follow His ways and acknowledged Him as king but rather Lucifer, then they will follow the sentence handed down to Lucifer for his rebellion against God, that being one thousand years in hell. The prize that we all are striving for at death is eternal life with God in heaven or eternal life with Lucifer in hell. You decide, not God. Take your pick.'

'The major component of man is his soul. The rest is his body, which physically protects the soul. It is an outer casing which you get to take care of. No surgeon can find your soul, operate on it, or touch it. Even if you have heart surgery. Two opposite influences, those being good and evil, control the soul. What the soul decides affects the body. For instance, if your soul decides it wants drugs or alcohol, then consumption of these substances will affect the body. The decision affects the soul, as I will explain later.'

'So where do we come from? Heaven. Why are we here? To serve God and, in the process, for our souls to be tested. Why? So mankind may have free choice and so that heaven will only contain those souls who have proven to be of the faith. The rest will end up in hell, as they are of no use to God. It is like buying a car, but the darn thing keeps breaking down or never runs. You get rid of it, so God is doing the same thing with those souls who have decided they prefer the way of this world instead of God's rule.'

'What is the test that is being applied? The test is your faith in Jesus Christ. Those souls who have faith in Jesus Christ will be the ones who go to or, may I say, are returned home to heaven. Those who declare Lucifer king will follow his fate – hell.'

'Now many ministers hammer the matter of faith to their congregation without really understanding it. How many times have you heard, "You should step forth and declare your faith in Jesus"? Or "You will go to hell if you do not have faith in Jesus"? How many times have you heard this? Faith, unfortunately, can't be something that is just declared as "Yes, I have faith in Jesus". Even though many say it, few have genuine faith. Mainly, it is a slogan or words that have a shallow foundation in most people.'

'The facts are that you were sent to Earth to serve God. You need to have faith in Him to do this. You need to believe in Him first to gain faith. To believe, you must have the Holy Spirit within you. To get the Holy Spirit, you must answer God's calling and respond, confirming you want a relationship with Him.'

'Genuine faith is something that is gained over time through fellowship with Jesus, where you begin slowly and progress to a point of trust in Jesus, even if the circumstances are dispiriting and, sometimes, life-threatening. We have heard that in the war, ministers and others have given up their lives for others, knowing that God will look after them. Others have died in the name of Christ. Their faith in Him makes this sacrifice worthwhile.'

'How is faith gained? This is a tough question to answer clearly, so stay with me on this one. You cannot even try to get faith without your soul first being called upon by God to follow Him. He will call you spiritually, not through your mobile. If you answer Him and declare that you wish to have fellowship with Him as you believe in Him, he will send the Holy Spirit to live within you. The Holy Spirit is from God and will guide you on your journey to faith.'

'After a period, the happening of events that will affect your soul will test your faith. These are called trials, and their purpose is twofold. First, they are to make you more like Christ, and second and most importantly, they allow you to judge for yourself whether you really have faith in the Lord. Many Christians say, "Lord, Lord," but how many of them truly say, "Lord, I disagree or cannot see where you are going or leading me, but I have faith in you, and Thy will, will be done"?

'The trials are compounded over a period which could be many years and become more intensive and personal as time goes by. If you continue, you will be tested to your limits.'

'Many a person thinks the trials are a sign that you are being tested by God or punished by Him. This is not true. They are designed for you to gain faith in Christ to where you know He will be there for you. You trust Him. They are designed to take away your doubts about Christ. They are to anchor your faith on rock and not on sand, which will be blown away by the first gust of wind.';

'As the years go on, the trials are compounded, become harder and more emotional to where you may end your belief in God for several reasons. For instance, your next-door neighbour may rape your six-year-old. Your immediate reaction is "Where was God? Surely, being a Christian amount to something. Why didn't He prevent this?" Of course, you will not blame yourself for not being a good parent and ensuring you knew where your daughter was at all times. No, no, it wasn't your fault. It was God's. What's the use of being a Christian if these things may happen?

'The true Christian will respond by saying, "Lord, I don't understand why this has happened, and my heart is heavy with sorrow, but while I can't understand or know of your plan, I believe in time, you will reveal this to me, and I accept you know best. Amen."

'As the trials evolve, they become longer and harder to accept. Your faith will be tested to the degree where you believe God has left you. You pray but don't feel His presence. You get no response from God and assume He has left you to your own devises. Lucifer is sent in to test you, as was the case with Adam and Eve. The doubts enter your mind, and you believe the only course of action is for you to decide rather than rely on God.'

'As time goes by, the problem compounds and doesn't get resolved. You despair, for in your mind, you know what it takes to set things right, but this just doesn't happen. You cannot fix the problem yourself and believe it is your fault or that you are a failure. You pray to the Lord, but your prayers are not answered, and it feels as if the Lord has walked out on you or He just doesn't care and doesn't want to know you or about your problems.'

'You resolve that the train speeding down the track towards you will not stop and will just run right over you, as you can't get out of the way. You believe God is playing chicken with your life and has miscalculated the situation. Either your faith leaves you at this point and you join the ranks of the disbelievers, or your faith is strengthened and you continue to trust the Lord, whatever happens. Even if it means death.'

'Some in this predicament try to bargain with the Lord. "Since you are having a difficult time in deciding on what you want, why don't you allow the following to happen? If you do, I will be a good Christian for the next three weeks or whatever." The bargaining never works. Only frustration and disbelief are achieved, as the Lord will not bargain with you. He will take you to your limits and then some. Your faith must be anchored in Him on solid rock, or you will lose it.'

This is not a game, but real life and the stress on you and your emotions will be extreme and disheartening.

'In reality, the Lord has not left you but is giving you space to see if you can work out how the problem should be resolved, according to you. He will then resolve the problem in His own way and in His time if you have faith in Him, giving you an opportunity to judge what He has done for you and compare His outcome to what you had contemplated for yourself. The emptiness that you felt also gives you some understanding of what Jesus felt when His Father turned from Him on the cross and the sorrow and emptiness He felt at that point in time.'

'You are not on your own in the feeling you have been let down during these trials. Job lost all of his family and his fortune and was given no explanation as to why. It was his belief in the Lord that proved everyone wrong, and the advice given to him was false and inaccurate. The Lord was testing his faith and allowed him to judge this for himself through extreme circumstances.'

'The story of Ruth tells us that a great famine came upon the land. They prayed to the Lord for His intervention and help. This did not come, and they finally decided that they must go to Egypt so they could get food and shelter their animals. When they arrived in Egypt, they invited Ruth to marry the pharaoh. It was not until the Lord had intervened that the whole family could escape from Egypt and return to their lands. While on the journey to Egypt, many of the household died through starvation and lack of water. Their faith was tested time after time in life-and-death situations.'

'The majority who are not Christians cannot experience these trials because they have said, "No, thank you. I have another god – me, money, sex, gambling, or anything I can't do without. I know better than you, and I have decided that I do not need you to meddle in my life. I don't want fellowship with the Lord. I am satisfied with what I have, and what you offer doesn't appeal to me. I need material things." The concentration here is self and only on self. These people cannot get eternal life but appear on the surface as getting the greater rewards or benefits this world can offer.

They don't go through trial as there is no point. They are not being groomed by Jesus, but by Lucifer. They are being trained or groomed for a different life than the one Jesus offers.

'It is at the time of death that closure appears, and they realise that they have, in reality, achieved nothing from their term on Earth. All that they have worked for, will go at death, for they cannot take anything with them. Those who have held the faith are gifted eternal life. Those who don't have faith in Jesus end up in hell with their king, Lucifer.'

'Lucifer is necessary to test mankind. Without him, there would be no one. God, being truth, could not introduce evil to test man and man as his prime creation, for the future must learn and experience faith in Jesus Christ. Without this, man is useless to God. He must experience what sin does to his soul and what it takes to regain a sin-free life through the cross. He must believe that there is a better life in heaven than the one on Earth. He must trust the teachings of Jesus. We have been made in His image and may stay in sin or ask for help to find a better way and a better future, one by faith.'

'Remember Christ in the desert, where Jesus refused Lucifer's offer? All he had to do was kneel before Lucifer and declare him king, but he didn't. The reason was that there are far better offerings in heaven than on this earth and that Lucifer was offering what was not his. He did not create the earth and man. God did. Lucifer, being the true salesman, was giving back to Jesus what was his, and since he failed, he now is trying to sell the same spiel to you.'

'If you reject Christ often enough, you become less inclined to seek fellowship with the Lord and, over time, drop your faith altogether. Each time you compromise your faith, you know it is contrary to the teachings of Christ, and once the decision is made, you will feel as if you have made the wrong one and meditate on it for some time. Your soul will ensure this happens. The Lord will continually try to influence your soul that you are doing wrong and get you to come back to Him. If you do, you recommence your trial. If you don't, then eventually, you will be on your own. The Holy Spirit will leave you and you will be on your own with Lucifer.'

'Many have left Christ to follow Lucifer, as they cannot accept the fact that Jesus has caused or allowed the trials to happen. They are lost forever. They forget Jesus has given you and all others the right of free choice. This, unfortunately, does allow your brother or sister the right to shoot you or run you down in their car or hurt you in many ways as part of their free choice. God will not interfere as all will account to him on Judgement Day. Others do come back and are accepted as a prodigal son returning.'

'Sin may come to you at the most unexpected time. For example, you are put in a compromising position, such as there is a promotion at work and an increase in salary. All you have to do is support the team and be one of them. However, the members of the team tell lies and have dubious practices which steal from their clients, such as banks charging unnecessary fees to clients or acting unethically. Or an insurance company billing fees to people who are deceased. All designed to defraud the customer. All for money, which, in reality, is their god. You know of these practices and have to decide whether you are following Christ, or will you kneel before Lucifer and declare him king and accept the promotion or the new job?'

'Now we come back to the present situation. Do you accept the offer, knowing it will compromise your belief and reject the truth, which is Christ? By accepting, you have basically declared you have no faith in Christ and accept Lucifer's proposal to you, which you believe is better and far more truthful than Christ's offer. Put in another way, the decision guaranteeing eternal life is outweighed by what is offered now to you on this earth, and you accept this offer.'

'By rejecting the offer, you have shown your faith in Christ and have put your life in His hands and recognize the liar Lucifer is. From here on, the road will be rough, and things could get tricky, but always, you will have the assurance of Christ's presence, and He will deliver you into a better situation or position than what you could have imagined. He will fight for you and protect you as you have showed to yourself by your action that you truly have faith and do not just speak the words. You have showed it. God knows what is in your heart. There will not be loneliness in you as you can always confide in Him, and He will be with you.'

'By accepting the offer presented to you and rejecting the truth, you move closer to Lucifer and further away from Christ. You become one of the team. Care should be taken, for the mob that you are with can turn on you at any time, and you can lose everything you connived to gain. Christ rode to Jerusalem on a donkey with the crowd yelling, "Hosanna! Hosanna!" on Palm Sunday, with all the friends one could ever want. One week later, the same mob was screaming, "Crucify Him!" The same thing may happen to you. By refusing to accept these practices and maintain your faith, you are assured no crowd will come after you, and every move will be for your benefit and not to your detriment. Lucifer will always do whatever it takes for you to reject Christ and, in turn, have the Holy Spirit move away from you. Once that happens, he has gained you, and it is unlikely you will ever be allowed to return to Christ.

'Many in our congregation believe in Jesus. Few have taken the risk and challenge of declaring or showing their faith in Him. The risk you no doubt believe is too high and to trust the Lord when you never have to is a colossal task. Most believe they can stay in their comfort zone without risking their assets or lifestyle. Tell that to the heart attack victims or those who have lost their possessions through fire, cyclones, or floods. When this happens, it is still rare to have a person give their life to Christ and have total faith in Him, even though they have nothing left.'

'I tell you that most of the population does not believe in Christ. I can count the number who have faith in Him on two hands. You see tests of faith happening every day. Your friends or mates tell you a dirty joke, and you laugh at it. "Good one." You are told some gossip and really don't know whether this is true, but you still pass it on. You are told to do something at work by a boss or manager, knowing it is wrong, but still do it. You are sold a watch or a computer at the pub, knowing that someone has stolen it.'

'The test of faith is ongoing until you don't care and no longer declare yourself a Christian or get to a point where you stand up for Christianity and do what is considered the right thing in the name of the Lord. This is one reason the Lord doesn't have another flood. It is to ensure you have whatever time that is necessary for you and not the Lord to find the way and declare your alliance to the Christian faith and the Lord and to enable the souls in heaven to come and be tested as you are.'

'Previously, I had experienced an emotional problem, and I could get through it with the help of the Lord. On other occasions, I relied on myself and, being a failure, fell in a heap and became depressed. The problem was bigger than I could manage, and I didn't have the skill or ability to handle it or resolve it on my own. No problem is too big or complicated for Christ to handle.'

'The non-Christian gets the support of the devil, who wants to gather an army of lost souls for the last confrontation when it comes. He believes that if he has a force of two to one against God, God will back off and not do what He has said He was going to do, namely, send them to hell along with all the other non-Christians.'

'Throughout the years, the non-Christian has been losing as more and more of the Western world upholds the Christian belief. To reverse this, the non-Christians introduced minority groups such as homosexuals and drug users, groups to delude the Christian faith. The church, instead of attacking the root cause of this turmoil, pulled the sheets over their heads and went to sleep. They should have made clear the purpose of Christianity and the difference between a believer and a non-believer and that the Christians would not accept the dilution of Bibles standards. Instead, they made a bolt for the hills, with the non-Christians left dictating the standards of the day, which are forever changing.'

'The Christian must battle on irrespective of the challenge and must maintain the teachings of the Bible, for they are not outdated as some would want you to believe, but are relevant today, as they were in Jesus's days. The bar is high and, in most cases, too high for the non-Christians, who, because they cannot attain those standards, try to have them removed from society.'

'You will be given several tests during your trials, as was Jesus in the wilderness. You will reach the point where you would like to say to God, "Turn these stones into bread." I urge you not to test the Lord but go to Him in prayer and ask for His help and strength. When you can take no more of the trials, you will be confronted with an opportunity that is too good to be true. A way which will let you out of your misery, a path to abundance. The only price you will have to pay is to kneel before Lucifer and acknowledge him as king. If you take his offer, your problems will be over. At that point, you would have, by your action, gained a new master. Be careful of Greeks bearing gifts, as the Holy Spirit will not remain with you if you have refused your faith continuously.'

'Some of you have come from another church where you have been told you are going to be judged by your good deeds and that's enough to get you eternal life. Well, it isn't for two reasons. First, your good deeds relate to the commandment of "Love thy neighbor as you would have them love you". Second, it will not give you the Holy Spirit, and without the Holy Spirit, you walk alone, not with God. You are not brought to Christ or tempted by trials. You don't have the faith in Jesus Christ, only in yourself, a poor substitute for the Creator. Most here have faith for one hour every Sunday. Thereafter, the world takes control, and you wonder where God is. You search your back pocket to see if He is there.'

'I urge you to stop being superficial. Pray to the Lord and ask Him to take you by the hand and begin your journey with Him, having faith, through good and bad, in Jesus Christ our Lord. Yes, He will take you through good and bad, but that is why you have been placed on Earth. Not for a sinful episode or a luxurious life, which reaches its "use by" date quickly. You have been placed on this earth to follow the ways of our Lord, to serve Him, to experience things that affect your soul, and to be made more like Christ. He will look after you and feed and clothe you, as He has done from the days of Adam and Eve.'

'I urge you not to bow before Lucifer. The gains he offers are of this world only and will not give you eternal life. Jesus, when offered the world by Lucifer, makes it clear that this is a poor substitute for what God offers you, and therefore, you should not throw away your future gain, for something very temporary and that would evaporate before your eyes when you try to secure it.'

'So to summarize the sequence before we move on, first, you are born in sin. God must approach you and seek His fellowship and accept His call to receive the Holy Spirit. Your belief in Christ will bring on the trials. You will undertake trials to strengthen your belief. These will be demanding and affect you spiritually and emotionally. You may renounce Christ but will be drawn back to Him. Have faith at all times.'

'When you find yourself in trouble, pray to the Lord. Most Christians do this after the event when they get home, not when the event happens. I say this because you have a free choice, and unless you exercise this, God will not involve Himself in your matter. The choice is yours. If you do not pray, he will know what is happening but will not interfere, assuming this is your desire. When you pray, you can tell the

Lord what has happened and ask for His help, which He will provide, but you must request it, as it is not automatically given. Continue your prayer throughout the problem, seeking guidance and the Lord's grace. When it is resolved, make sure you thank the Lord for all He has done.'

'Remember when ten lepers approached the Lord and asked for His help and He made them clean and took their leprosy away? Only one came back and thanked Him, and he was an outsider. The Lord said, "Your faith has healed you."'

Chapter 15

Simon was out in his front yard, watering his garden, enjoying the peace, when he noticed a car pull up in front of his house, and a woman stepped out of the driver's side and a younger woman from the passenger's side.

The older woman walked up to Simon and asked, 'Are you the minister?'

Simon said, 'Yes, what can I do for you?'

'My name is Nancy, and this is my daughter, Sarah. We would like to have a quick word with you. My daughter is insisting, but I believe it is a waste of time.'

Simon looked at the daughter and could see she was under stress and crying. He stopped watering and turned off the tap and said, 'I believe we can talk more privately inside. Would you care to come into the house?'

Simon opened the door and led the two into the lounge. At the same time, Monique came out of the bathroom after taking a shower, wrapped in just a loose towel. She stopped and gave a scream, thinking an intruder was in the house. She noticed Simon was standing near the woman and stared at them for a moment, trying to fathom why they were in her house. The two women stared at Monique, and everyone was speechless. Monique turned and went into the bedroom and closed the door.

Simon said, 'That was my wife, Monique.'

Nancy replied, 'I bet.'

'Can I get you a drink?'

'No, we didn't come here for afternoon drinks. We want to get our problem resolved.'

Monique came out of the bedroom. 'Sorry I screamed, I wasn't expecting anyone to be in the lounge. I just had a shower after working in the garden. Please sit down.'

Simon asked Nancy, 'Now what is this all about?'

Nancy explained, 'This prostitute of a daughter has got herself pregnant. We went to see Peter Sutherland at St Andrews Church, who told us that under the circumstances, it would be all right for Sarah to have an abortion. She doesn't believe him and wants a second opinion. I think it is a waste of time, and who cares what the church thinks? She should book herself into a clinic and get it done as quick as possible.'

'So, Nancy, you are advocating an abortion. The quicker, the better. But what I gather is Sarah doesn't know or doesn't believe she should abort the pregnancy. Is that right?'

'If she goes ahead with the pregnancy, people will laugh at us and say that we have brought up a daughter who doesn't know how to keep her legs closed. We will be the laughingstock of the street. The parents of a prostitute.'

'So, Nancy, you want your daughter to have the abortion, so your friends and neighbours won't make comments to you about your daughter and her predicament? Is that right?'

'She is an embarrassment to us all. There is no alternative. The child will be a bastard. Our family and friends will make comments behind our backs, and everyone will laugh at us, saying we haven't brought her up right.'

Simon said, 'Sarah, what do you think? What do you want to do?'

Sarah said, while trying to keep the tears back, said, 'It's not my mother's decision.' She sniffed. 'It's mine, and frankly, I don't trust that Peter Sutherland. He will say anything for money. I don't believe he knows what the Bible says or has ever read one. He will tell you what is convenient and not the truth.'

Nancy said, 'You only object to what he said because it is the truth. Get it straight. No one wants a child out of wedlock.'

'I, unlike my mother, consider myself a Christian. I believe in Jesus and don't think He wants me to kill my unborn child.'

'Get it through your head. You are not killing anyone. The child hasn't been born. The law lets you abort the pregnancy, and no one will know of your predicament. You can get on with your life as if nothing had happened.'

Simon said, 'I am not sure what Mr. Sutherland has told you. But it is a sin to have an abortion. The church views this as if you are killing an unborn baby. Life is within you, and you have been given a gift that cannot be manufactured, bought, or reproduced. It is a creation from God given to you, Sarah, and you, Nancy, want to kill it because you are worrying what the neighbours will think.'

Nancy said, 'It's not a human. It's nothing, only nine weeks old. Doctors don't consider it to be life, just a body in development.'

'That's totally wrong. If you see an ultrasound of a baby at this stage, you will see it has a heart and limbs that are being developed. It, therefore, is alive and is a child. It has a heartbeat. You can see blood is being pumped around the body. The only difference is it has not fully developed, which will take nine months. To end the pregnancy is the same as killing a child.'

'Good riddance to it, I say. We don't need the problem or another mouth to feed.'

Monique, who was standing and listening to the conversation, sat next to Simon. Monique asked, 'You're scared, aren't you, Sarah? Not of the birth, but what your mother has been saying and no doubt trying to run your life.'

Nancy said, 'She can't be trusted on her own. Look what has happened to her. Her father doesn't want to speak to her, saying that if this is the way she wants to live her life, then she should get out of the house and live on her own, away from them. He doesn't want anything to do with her. He calls her a f——ing prostitute.'

Simon said, 'I think that's going a bit too far.'

Monique suggested, 'I think I should call Frances and see if she can come over.'

Simon agreed. 'That's a good idea. Frances is part of a group in our church who help girls in Sarah's situation. She is a trained midwife and has worked at the local hospital before retiring.'

Nancy retorted, 'I don't need another person involved. She is having an abortion, and that's that. It may be a sin, and it may be against God's commandments, but He is going to get over it. This girl is going to have an abortion, and that's that.'

A voice was heard from outside. 'Like hell she is. It's people like you who only care about themselves and not Sarah. It's what you want and not what is right. All you can think about is you, and you don't care about our child.'

The front doors opened, and a young man in his early twenties came in. He introduced himself as Tim.

Tim said, 'I was driving past and saw Nancy's car out the front and thought she may be here with Sarah. I am glad I came in and overheard what she was saying.'

Nancy said, 'Haven't you caused us enough problems? Get out. No one asked you in.'

Tim raised his voice. 'It should be you who gets out, not me. It is my baby, not yours. We will work out what must be done, not you. So go home and leave us alone. You don't care about the baby or what the termination may do to us mentally or physically.'

'But I do. It will ensure that you stay away and that we will never see you again. This should be your problem, not ours. You had the thirty-second ride, jockey, and we now have to shoot the horse to get to clean up your mess.'

Nancy got up and stomped out of the house, got into her car, and drove off without saying a word. There was a knock at the door, and Monique went to see who was there. She opened the door.

Monique said, 'Hi, Frances. Thanks for coming over on such short notice.' She took Frances into the lounge, where Sarah was sitting. 'Sarah, this is Frances from our church. She has helped a lot of young people get their lives together when an unexpected pregnancy arises. Frances, this is Sarah and Tim. Sarah is pregnant, and her mother, who just left, wants her to have an abortion. Her father is not speaking to her and has kicked her out of his house, and she is terrified as to what she should do. Peter Sutherland has advised Nancy and Sarah that there is no problem with them having an abortion, and Nancy believes him as it fits in with her plans.'

Frances said, 'It's criminal, what that man is doing, disguising as a minister of religion. He really is an antichrist. Well, Sarah, Tim, what do you want to do?'

Tim replied, 'I want Sarah to come home with me and live at our house and have the baby. My parents know about the pregnancy, and while they are disappointed in me, they will support us in any way they can. They have known Sarah for years since she was in preschool with me and think of her as a daughter.'

'I don't think that is a good idea right now. Sarah is upset and needs some time to think about her situation. My recommendation is that Sarah come home to my house and stay with me for a while until she sorts things out. I have a spare room and live in the house by myself. I will enjoy some company. We will go to her home tomorrow and explain things to her parents and get some clothes for her. What do you think, Sarah?'

Sarah said, 'That sounds the best thing to do. It will give us time to seek things out and for us to get our lives in order.'

Tim asked, 'You are going to have the baby, aren't you?'

'I didn't think Mr. Sutherland was telling us the truth, and I will not allow my baby to be killed or my pregnancy ended by a man when God has given me a life to take care of. I don't want a life like my mother's, where everything is dictated by my father, who is a control freak who becomes violent if you oppose him. It is his way or get out. I don't believe she really wants me to have an abortion, but it is what he wants while I am under his roof, and I have nowhere to go and no money to support myself. I can only find casual work and don't earn much as a waitress.'

'Come home with me. I will support both of us. We can get married.'

'That's what I am saying. I don't want to make a decision I will regret later on. Married, not on an apprentice's wage? No, I will go with Frances and stay a day or two and try to sort things out in my mind.'

Simon said, 'I will call in tomorrow after work to see how you are getting on.'

Frances said, 'All right. We better be going.'

Frances and Sarah walked to Frances's car, got in, and drove off.

Tim asked, 'What should I do?'

Simon replied, 'Wait and see. There is no rush. Let Sarah have some space and time. Otherwise, all she will do is swap one control freak for another.'

'I guess you are right. Unfortunately, she sees me as an elder brother rather than a potential husband.'

'Normal elder brothers don't have sex with their sisters. There may be some truth in what you say. The difference will be how you support her emotionally as to how you are going to be viewed.'

'I think you're right. I'll touch base with you on the weekend.'

'All right. By the way, Tim, what do you do for a living?'

'I am an apprentice electrician in my last year. It is a good job, but the firm I am working with doesn't do things as they should be done. Quick and nasty. It's the money that counts, not the quality of work or safety. I will see you later.'

Tim turned, walked out, got in his car, and drove off.

Simon said, 'And to think all I wanted to do was water my garden.'

Monique said, 'I'll start dinner while you finish the watering.'

Monique walked out and went into the kitchen, and Simon went back to his garden.

Chapter 16

Half an hour later, Frances pulled up outside her house, and Sarah got out of the car and followed Frances into her house.

Frances said, 'Well, this is it. I will show you to your room. There is the bathroom, and I have some old clothes that will fit you, so you can shower tomorrow morning.' Frances went to her cupboard and pulled out a shirt and a pair of jeans. She went into her room and came out with some underwear and a bra. 'This will fit you. I'll start dinner. I am sure you are hungry.'

Sarah said, 'I'll come and help.'

'Good. Mashed potatoes and sausages.'

'Sounds good. Where are the potatoes? I'll start peeling them.'

Frances opened the cupboard door, and Sarah grabbed some potatoes. She opened a couple of draws until she found the peeler and began peeling the potatoes. Frances switched the stove on, went to the fridge, got some sausages, took out a fry pan from the cupboard, and placed it on the stove.

Frances said, 'It smells good.'

Sarah said, 'I'll set the table.'

Frances finished cooking, mashed the potatoes, made the gravy, and put everything on the plates Sarah had set out.

Both sat down, and Frances said, 'Father, we thank you for the food we are about to receive. In your holy name, amen.'

Both began eating.

Frances asked, 'Does it taste all right?'

Sarah nodded and cut up one of her sausages and ate slowly, thinking about the events of the day. Sarah said, 'I can't go home now. My parents are against me. I will have to find a place to live. I really don't feel comfortable living with Tim, even though he is the father of my baby. I look at him as an elder brother, not as a husband. He has always been there for me.'

Frances said, 'No hurry, dear. You can stay here for a while until you know what you want to do.'

They finished their meal, and both cleared the table and washed the dishes and put things away. Sarah went into her room to lie down, while Frances went into the lounge to watch television. After one hour, Sarah came out of her room and watched television with Frances. Frances tried to switch channels to find a movie or show that did not have foul language or was about sex, but gave up and left the television on *How to Train Your Dragon*. At about ten o'clock, they switched the television and lights off, and both went to bed.

The next morning, they got up and had their showers and breakfast and went shopping. Both got in Frances's car and drove off to the shopping centre.

Tim had been working since seven thirty, rewiring a factory with a team of electricians. His job was to run out the cables, which he completed.

The senior team member went to the loudspeaker and broadcasted, 'Attention. I will cut the power off in five minutes. There will be no power for the next half hour.'

After five minutes, the head sparky checked whether everyone was off the circuit and cut the power at the fuse box. He put a sign on the box saying the power was off and that electricians were working on the electrical network.

Roy was employed as a factory hand. He was disabled but still able to follow orders. As a child, he had Down syndrome and found schooling hard to cope with. He was employed to work as an assistant to the sheet metal workers, who operated the guillotines and metal benders. He was partly deaf, owing to the refusal to wear earmuffs when he was around the machines.

Roy was in the toilet when the broadcast about cutting the power off was made, so he was not concentrating on what they said about the power being cut off for half an hour. He noticed no one was around and knew that there was an important job that had to be rushed through and completed today. So he decided to set up his guillotine and try to cut the sheet by himself. They left the key in the guillotine so there would be no problems. He put the sheet of metal on the deck of the guillotine, measured the size he needed to cut, locked in his safety barrier, and pressed the control to cut the sheet of metal, but nothing happened. He tried again. Despite that, nothing happened.

Roy remembered this had happened once before, and it was a fuse problem. He went to the switchboard and noticed a sign with writing on it. He couldn't read, so he looked for someone to read the sign and tell him what it said, but everyone was in the lunchroom having an early lunch. No one had told him what was happening, and most of the men treated him as an idiot rather than looking out for him or trying to train him. He wanted to finish his job, so he looked around and noticed the master switch was in an off position. He pushed it up into an on position, closed the switch box, went back to his machine, and cut his piece of metal.

The team was ready to replace some of the old wiring that had previously caused the machines to trigger the fuse box to switch the power off when it sensed a fault. The boss yelled out to Tim to cut the old wire and strip it from its cradle, which held it.

Tim grabbed his pliers and cut into the wire. He then gave a loud scream and shook as the voltage went through him and was thrown off his ladder onto the factory floor with such force that his head was partly dislocated from his body. All the workmen ran up to him, but they could see that he was in a bad way.

The boss yelled out, 'Which f——ing idiot turned the power on?' and ran to the master switch. He noticed his sign was on the floor and the master switch was on. He switched it off and yelled out, 'Power off!' and tapped the switch and closed the box. 'Has anyone called for an ambulance?'

One man yelled out, 'Yes, about five minutes ago! They're here!'

The paramedics ran up to Tim and yelled out, 'Is the power off?'

The boss replied, 'Yes, and the master switch tapped in an off position!'

One paramedic took this scope out of his bag to check for a heartbeat. After a few seconds, he yelled out, 'No pulls! He's dead! We will have to report this to the police!' The paramedic went back to his ambulance and picked up the radio. 'Base, we have attended the industrial accident and have found a man dead at the scene. Please inform the police, and we will stay around until they arrive.'

The policed arrived about ten minutes later and began to investigate what had happened and who was at fault. They advised all men to remain on site, and no one was to leave without first giving their details to an officer. They checked the body and noted the distance Tim was thrown from his ladder. Photographs were taken, and they made measurements.

The paramedics placed Tim's body in a body bag after the police had given permission and loaded it into the ambulance. They gave their details to the police and drove off to the morgue.

The boss said, 'I better go and tell Tim's parents their boy won't be coming home.'

Chapter 17

The manager of the installation drove to Tim's home and parked outside. He was confused about what he should say, as he had never done this before in his life. He was nervous and scared he would say the wrong thing.

He walked up to the front door and hesitated, thinking maybe he should leave this up to the police. No, he decided, Tim was part of his team, and he should be the one to tell his parents of the tragedy. He rang the doorbell and waited.

After about half a minute, a man appeared at the door and said, 'Yes, can I help you?'

The manager said, 'I am sure you can. Are you Mr. Jones, Tim's father?'

'Yes. What trouble has Tim got himself into?'

'Sir, can I come in? I need to speak to you?'

'Yes, by all means.'

Mr. Jones led the manager into the house and introduced him to his wife. Both stood waiting for the manager to tell them what he had to say.

Mr. Jones asked, 'Well, what is it you want to tell us?'

The manager said, 'I am sorry to inform you that there has been an accident at work, and Tim will not be coming home.'

'Why not?'

'He was electrocuted this morning and died at the scene. It was an industrial accident, and we couldn't revive him.'

Mrs. Jones burst into tears and became hysterical, yelling out, 'My only son! Lord, it can't be! Please, no, Lord, no!'

Tim's father tried to calm her down but could not and called for the ambulance. The ambulance arrived quickly and, upon being told what had happened, tried to give Mrs. Jones a sedative, but this did no good. They sedated her and took her to the hospital, as she was in shock. They got a sedative from their medical bag, and one paramedic held Mrs. Jones down in a chair, while the other inserted a needle into her arm. Within a few minutes, they released her as she was asleep. They got the stretcher from the ambulance, placed Mrs. Jones on it, and put her in the ambulance.

Mr. Jones, shocked at what had happened, said, 'I am coming with you to the hospital.'

He got his wallet and keys in the house, thanked the manager for coming and advising them of what had happened, got his telephone number and contact details so he could contact him later on, closed the front door, and got into the ambulance with his wife.

The ambulance sped off to the hospital. It arrived and took Mrs. Jones directly to the emergency ward. The doctors assessed her and kept her sedated and reduce the dosage during the day. The doctors hooked her up to the monitors so they could monitor her blood pressure and oxygen level. Tim's father sat by his wife's bed, not sure what they were going to do without Tim, who was their only child.

Meanwhile, Sarah and Frances had finished their shopping and were on their way back home when Frances received a message from the hospital, asking if she could ring them to advise of her availability next week as a volunteer.

Sarah said, 'What do you do at the hospital? I thought you retired as a nurse.'

Frances replied, 'I did, but once or twice a week, I volunteer to help people who come to the hospital who don't know what to do or where to go. I help them fill out their forms or direct them to the department they are looking for or the ward they are seeking and give general advice about which doctor is on duty if they have a specific medical problem.'

'That sounds interesting.'

'You mean tiring, don't you? But it keeps me active. It's better than staying home every day by yourself. It helps the community, and it helps my mental state. Look, we are just passing the hospital. I'll pull in and just see what days they need covered, if that is all right with you. It won't take too long.'

'No, that's all right. You do what you have to do. If you don't mind, I will come with you to see what the atmosphere is like. I don't want to be on my own.'

'Come along. It won't take long.'

Frances drove into the hospital staff car park but could not find a parking spot. It seemed a busy day. She drove to the emergency, where she parked her car and told the attendant who knew her well that she would only be a minute. Both ladies got out of the car, and Frances led the way through emergency to get to administration. As they walked through the emergency ward, Sarah was taken aback by the number of people who were there and then spotted Tim's father sitting near a bed with his head in his hands, somewhat crying.

Sarah said, 'Frances, there is Tim's father. Something is wrong. Can we go over to him to find out what's happened?'

Frances said, 'By all means. It most probably is nothing serious.'

They walked up to where Tim's father was, and Sarah touched him on the shoulder. She noticed Tim's mother lying in bed. She was not moving.

Sarah asked, 'Mr. Jones, what has happened to Mrs. Jones?'

Mr. Jones looked up and, with tears in his eyes, burst out, 'It's not Mrs. Jones, love. It's Tim. He's dead!'

Upon hearing what Mr. Jones had said, Sarah grabbed her stomach and gave out a yell, and fell to the floor. Frances quickly reached out and hit the red emergency button at the head of the bed, and the siren went off. Doctors and nurses quickly came running up to Sarah and checked her heartbeat, which was raised. They quickly put her into a bed and placed her on oxygen. She came around, still gripping her stomach.

The screen was drawn around her, and a gynecologist was called to emergency. Within minutes, the gynecologist examined Sarah and sent her off for an ultrasound examination. Sarah was taken to radiology, and they performed the ultrasound. The technician sent the report directly to the doctor's email, and Sarah was taken wheeled back to emergency.

After a few minutes, the gynecologist came to Sarah's bed and drew the screen, and examined Sarah. He lifted her dress and noticed the bleeding on her underpants. Frances immediately knew what had happened. Sarah had a miscarriage. She had lost her baby.

The doctor confirmed what Frances already knew and said that Sarah would have to stay in hospital for a few days to undergo some procedures. Frances went to Mr. Jones and gave him the bad news. He was uncontrollable to the extent that they had to sedate him as well.

Over the next two days, they brought Mrs. Jones out of her sedation, but she still could not accept that Tim had been taken from her and that she had also lost her grandchild. She was in a daze and kept saying to herself, 'What's the use of living when your family is taken from you?'

Mr. Jones was also brought out of sedation and accepted that his son Tim was dead and that he had also lost his grandchild. Both stayed in hospital for a further day for observation and were told that they could go home and prepared to leave the hospital. They called a taxi and were driven home to a house that seemed empty now that Tim had gone.

Sarah had completed her procedures, and the pain had gone, but not the hurt and heartache. The doctors agreed she could go home but wanted her to come back for a check-up in a month's time. She sat waiting for her discharge papers when, suddenly, Frances came up to her bed.

Frances asked, 'How are we today?'

Sarah replied, 'All right, I guess. Just can't stop worrying about the Joneses and what the two deaths are going to do to them. You know, when I was young, I spent more time at their place than I did at my home. They always treated me as their daughter, and I had my bedroom at their house. They are really nice people and deserve better out of life than what they are getting.'

'Yes, I agree, but I can't give them that life.'

'But I can. I can look after them if they will allow me.'

'Only one way to find out. Ask them.'

Sarah paused for a minute and stared into emptiness and then said, 'Frances, will you drive me to their house?'

Frances answered, 'Of course I will. Let's get going.'

They both walked to Frances's car and got in. Frances started the car and drove off.

After about thirty minutes, Frances stopped outside the Jones's house and said, 'Do you want me to go in with you?'

Sarah replied, 'No, it will be all right.'

Sarah got out of the car and walked slowly up to the front door, not knowing what to expect. She rang the doorbell and waited. She could hear someone coming to the door, and then it was opened, and Mr. Jones stepped out.

Mr. Jones said, 'Sarah, love, what brings you here? Not more bad news, I hope. God only knows we couldn't take any more.'

Sarah asked, 'Where is Mrs. Jones?'

'She is lying down. She doesn't feel herself.'

'Can I come in?'

'Of course you can. You know you used to live here once.'

'That's what I want to talk to you about. I know the house feels empty without Tim, and I was wondering whether you could use a border. Someone whom you know.'

Mrs. Jones came out of the bedroom and stood at the doorway for a moment and then made a move towards Sarah. With that, Sarah moved towards Mrs. Jones, and both hugged each other.

Mrs. Jones said, 'Welcome home, Sarah.'

Sarah said, 'Thanks, Mum.'

Chapter 18

S imon said to the congregation, 'Following last week's sermon, I have decided this Sunday to continue to explain the factual aspects of the Bible rather than get involved with interpreting the scriptures, which we will get into in the coming weeks.'

'The sermon this Sunday is about your relationship with God and why you seek him. Many have difficulty grasping this, as I have noted from discussions with you. I don't intend to cover the qualities of God, as most of you know He is everywhere and is an all-knowing, loving God and is capable of all things. Who is God? God is the God of Abraham, Isaac, and Jacob. He is the God of Noah and Moses. He is the God who took His people out of Egypt and across the Red Sea. He is then the God who performed many miracles through Jesus Christ, including the resurrection.'

'Yet many still will not accept Christ and try their utmost to belittle the Christian faith as if they fear it. The attitude is to wipe it off the face of the earth and replace it with a man-made alternative. God has given man the freedom to decide what they wish out of life. A life limited to the existence of this world or eternal life under the teaching of Jesus Christ. You cannot have both. Unfortunately, the debate and teaching are one-sided, with the voice of the Christian rarely heard.'

'When you have had enough of this world, its lies and cheating, its frauds and dishonesty, its norm, then find a small space for yourself and say a brief prayer to Jesus. "God, I have failed and need your help. Please take my soul and put me on the path of righteousness. Amen." I ask you, what happens when you lie, cheat, murder, have sex with your secretary, and such? At the crucifixion, there was one criminal to the left of Christ and one to the right of Him. The one on the right had faith in Jesus, while the one on the left did not. He was an agent of the devil.

'The principle of opposing forces – POF – shows itself at the cross. The confrontation we speak of here is confronting truth with falsehood, lies, murder, rape, and such. The principle of opposing forces is truth on the right and falsehood on the left. The denial of the truth is the same as falsehood and is a movement to the left under POF. Each left and right arm has degrees ranging from one to ten, with one being shallow and ten being extreme.'

'When your soul is touched by Jesus and you accept His calling and begin fellowship with Him, you move to the right. As your faith is confirmed through belief and trials, you move farther along the scale till you reach a point of seven, when it is unlikely you will give away your belief entirely and never return to the Christian faith. It is possible for you to slip back to three right or even three left. It is at the point of nine and ten right that you have total faith in the Lord and that your faith is cemented into rock. At point one, you are on sand, which is continually shifting.'

'Belief alone is not enough to gain eternal life. As stated, many believe, but few have faith in Jesus and ask Him to direct their lives. Most members of the congregation believe in Jesus, but only a few will have total faith in Him to allow Him to direct their lives. This also applies to movements to the left. As you move to ten left, you become more and more locked into the way of this world and Lucifer and are less inclined to accept Christianity or have faith in Christ, and you become a servant of the devil, Lucifer.'

'You begin on the POF path, moving left and right from the day you can comprehend the difference between good and evil. As you sin, you move left, and when you follow the ways of Jesus, you move right. If you sin and continue along this path, you will basically say, "I no longer have faith in Christ and His teachings," and at about point seven, you kneel before Lucifer and declare him king. Once you pass seven, it will be rare for a person to reclaim their spirituality and faith in Christ. They are lost forever, and at that point, the Holy Spirit will depart from them and no longer live within their soul. You are on your own.'

'The tug of war is happening every minute of every day until you reach a point where you believe what is best for you, which could take many years or a lifetime of moving back and forth from left to right. Each morning, when you rise, you begin the day at the point you left off the previous day. You do not go back to neutral. Moving left tends, in most cases, to be easy, and the devil entices you through prizes, better jobs, promotions, sex, money, temporary things. Regaining movement to the right takes recognition of Christ, what He stands for, and willingness to follow His ways, believe in Him, and request His forgiveness.'

'Many make the movement left and right, and many continually sin to the degree that they are between seven and ten on the left. I believe that most of the population would be between three and five left. It is rare for Christians to get to seven right, let alone to reach ten, which is of total faith on solid rock and this includes ministers of religion.'

'At this point, we must accept the premise that Christ is truth. When Christ was arrested and taken before the Pharisees for interrogation, Peter, one of the disciples, was waiting outside. They challenged him as being a friend of Jesus, and he denied knowing Him. What he did was to deny the truth. If he had faith in Christ, he would not deny Him. He knew who He was but could not comprehend how the ruler of the universe could be chained, arrested, and brought before the Pharisees for questioning. He denied Jesus because he did not have faith that He was the true Messiah. We are told that later on, it dawned upon Peter what he had done, and no doubt he thought of the time when he had seen Jesus, Moses, and Elijah on the mountain in the transformation, realized he was wrong, and wept.'

'The first thing that must be understood is that God the Father will not accept nor tolerate sin. They threw Lucifer out of heaven as they found him to be a sinful angel, not willing to repent and follow the ways of God. In fact, he wanted to be above God and rule both heaven and earth. With him went a third of the angels in heaven, and they established a stronghold on Earth and rule it now.'

'Mankind, who was created in the image of God, became separated from God when Adam and Eve sinned against God. From that point on, mankind was born into sin and needed to accept the death of Jesus Christ on the cross so he can, through Jesus, again have a relationship with God. Jesus took our sins to the cross, enabling those who believe in Him to be in the presence of God and not be separated from Him and have eternal life. Those who remain in sin will follow the path of Lucifer and go to hell.'

'God created mankind to serve the Lord and not oneself. Yet many have not noted this key factor, and they do as they please to satisfy their needs, to accumulate wealth in this world at any cost. This is their prime aim in life for them and not the concern of eternal life or Jesus Christ or the fact that we are here on a mission, temporarily. They ignore that this is a high price to pay just to satisfy "self" on this earth.

'Some ministers believe that the best way of describing the difference between the two opposing forces is to consider what is being proclaimed.

With the left movement, you basically are dealing with "self" and reflecting the image of Lucifer. It was Lucifer who wanted to be above God, and it was for him personally and not the good of all that he turned against God. So when you reject the gospel and Christ, you are basically saying, "It is for *me*. That's why I am doing this. Like Lucifer, I can be above God". Cain killed Abel for his own personal reason. For his "self", thinking, "If Abel is out of the way, it will be better for me, and there will be no opposition to me." The self is the governing principle here. The self is the way of Lucifer, and it was Lucifer who had convinced Cain to kill Abel. The Bible describes Lucifer as a murderer, whereas God is for the good of all and is described as the good shepherd.

'We hear throughout the world the massacres of innocent people by an individual or group of individuals shooting the innocent for no apparent reason. While this is a complicated area and there are many theories provided by expert psychiatrists and psychologists, one thing that comes out of the questioning from those perpetrators who live to tell is that it is for self-notoriety. They say it is for a cause, but the reality is that within the person, there is need of recognition, and to get this, they must do a hideous act which is perpetrated on a larger number of innocent people so they can get the attention of the world news and broadcasters for their act to be recognized. This "self" is characteristic of Lucifer and no doubt with his approval.'

'Lucifer works through man to achieve his ends. With Adam and Eve, it was by a talking snake. With terrorist activity, it is through ideology, or a sick mind being manipulated. Using these disguises, substitutes or means prevents the average person declaring the works to be at the hand of Lucifer, and his anonymity is preserved. Those who take delight in refusing the teaching of Christianity in schools and other places and mock Christian beliefs should stand up and declare that they have been part of the cause of these incidences as the fabric of society is eroded every time they legislate contrary to the teachings of the Bible and in accordance with modernity.'

'Many Christians have their own version of Christ and own interpretation of the Bible. It is the traditional Christian who has faith in God, as noted in the Bible, and because of their faith, they will have eternal life. The rest will find they have missed the mark and end up in hell as they move left along the scale to ten left.'

'Many academics argue the acceptance of Jesus but separate him from Christ. They accept He was a person on this earth but do not accept He was God's son and that he performed His miracles in the name of the Father. From our perspective, He is Jesus Christ, who died for our sins as Jesus Christ, and rose to heaven as Jesus Christ. The Bible does not separate Jesus from Christ. Nor should we. The play of words should stay with the academics and not be aired to the populace.'

'The next point to consider is your personal relationship with God. To describe this, I would like you to cast your mind back to when your children were born. I ask you truthfully, who was the boss? We all know the newborn baby was. As soon as it cried, you came running in to check on it. If it needed a feed, you provided it immediately. If it wanted its nappy changed, well, this mainly was left to the wife, but it was done reasonably quickly. So is it with God. If we need something, He will attend to it. He may not give you what you have asked for, but it will be something far better. However, it may not be immediately as it must fit within his plan.'

'When you attained the age of being able to distinguish between good and evil – truth and falsehood – one important thing happened in your life. God stepped back and gave you space to start your life unprotected. Without His spirit protecting you from the forces of evil, Lucifer moves in to fill the gap and to claim you as his own as you are born in sin. God has given you the freedom of choosing the type of life you end up with, and the only way you can do this is to experience good and evil, and throughout your life, you felt more comfortable with one of these and eventually join forces with them. God continually calls you, and when you hear His voice and believe in Him, He will send the Holy Spirit to dwell in you and assist you to move closer to Him and gain faith in Him.'

'God gives you space because the decision is ultimately yours, a God-given right to all mankind. The Holy Spirit is there to guide you and to prevent Lucifer from taking immediate possession of your soul, as he will try to do. Remember, Lucifer's intention is to get you on his side, and he will do anything necessary to achieve this. He will not give you an opportunity to think about it or defer your decision later. He will be right on top of you, shrouding you with worldly gifts to ensure you do not depart from him. A good sign of his presence is when things come your way, relatively without effort by you or expense to you. A promotion, a lottery win, an opportunity or a prize. If you try to refuse him or move away from him, he will bring you back by either discrediting you or your reputation or trying to put thoughts or doubt in your mind, as he did to Eve. The same thing happened to Jesus when he was in the desert for forty days. Lucifer appeared before him and showed him all the major cities of the world and said he would give them to Jesus. All he had to do was bow before him and declare him king. And now he is asking you to do it with the same test and gifts.'

'God will remain at a distance from you every day unless you ask Him to come closer and have Him help you with your life. He gives you total control of your life and does not rush in to confuse you or to urge you to make a hasty decision. If you want God to be with you daily, then advise Him that this is your wish, and He will be with you throughout the day.'

'Your relationship with God is tested when one partner dies and the other is left on their own. Many of our parishioners have advised me of the loneliness they have felt when their husband or wife, or even their son or daughter, dies after living together for many years. The feeling described in some ways is the feeling Christ felt on the cross when the Father turned from Him. It is emptiness and sorrow that is heart-wrenching, and you basically do not know what to do but cry.'

'Many have not experienced this feeling yet but will during their life. Jesus experienced it on the cross, and you will feel this in your lifetime. Those who are not Christians will find it hard to fill the gap. They will try to fill the emptiness by attaching to another person, but this rarely takes away the hurt that is felt. Those who are Christians can seek help from the Lord, and He will comfort you and be with you always. He doesn't come for a visit and then leave to go home. He is there for you, with you.'

'As you look around in a quiet moment, you see your departed loved one sitting in their old chair or lying on their bed or standing near a table, looking at you, and then you realise your mind is playing tricks on you. They, unfortunately, are in your thoughts, but not your presence. I ask all to recognize the loss and help those who have lost loved ones during this emotional period.'

'You can guarantee that those who do not believe in Jesus will not find comfort or an answer to their grief. They cannot turn to Jesus as they do not believe in Him. They will conclude that there is no God, as there is no instant resolution to their problem. They call upon God, but He will not answer them, and they will be as empty after the event as they were before the event. Unfortunately, their god – namely, themselves – is as deaf as a doorpost. They do not recognize that they only believe in themselves, and they cannot fix their problem.'

'Another aspect I wish to cover is one's attitude to God. Some seem to think that God is their friend or buddy. He is not and should not be referred to as such. He is neither and should be respected as what He is. The Creator and our God. Others, unfortunately, run on the rent-a-God principle, where they remember God on Sunday for an hour or two, and thereafter, it is back to running their lives according to their desires or wishes. They pay homage to God during church service, sing a few songs for Him, and go home and never think about God until the next Sunday. In between the Sundays, they believe they are Christians as they know of God and go to church on Sundays. What more do you want?'

'You ask where the rent side of it comes in. Well, as they passed the plate around, they place in the plate an amount that they consider equal to the benefit they have received during that week. If they have had a terrible week, then rent-a-God hasn't performed for them, and therefore, a small amount is put on the plate. If they have had a wonderful week, then a bit more is tossed in. Mind you, not too much more. We don't want to overdo it now, do we?'

'The other area where a person has a relationship with God is when they marry and consummate their marriage. At the time of marriage, each partner, assuming they are Christians, has the Holy Spirit living in them with their soul. When the marriage is consummated, the couple becomes one in that there is only one Holy Spirit for that marriage, not two as when they were single. If, over time, the couple divorces for non-biblical reasons, then they do not revert to a two–Holy Spirit position. They stay as they were with, say, half a Holy Spirit in each of them. With half a Holy Spirit, there is little doubt that the devil will come knocking at their door, and in a vulnerable situation, they may begin their movement left and not look back.'

'Should either party meet up with another person and marry them, the Holy Spirit will again become half upon consummation of that marriage. If, after a time, they split up again, the Holy Spirit in them is further diluted, and if this trend continues, as has been reported with the rich and famous, the Holy Spirit becomes diluted to the point of extinction in that person, and they lose their contact with Christ. Without the Holy Spirit, they cannot have eternal life and are doomed to hell at death, irrespective of their beliefs. Lucifer fills the hole from this point, and the person is lost to Christ. So the relationship with God and the gaining of faith is not something that you can gamble with or take lightly or deem that it will always be on call when you want it.'

'We have heard in the press that throughout the world, ministers have molested children and have used them for their own gratification. Many have taken these opportunities to again attack religion and, in particular, the Christian religion. While we recognized these as abhorrent acts, they are acts of men and not of God, and therefore, these men should pay for their crimes. God has already been crucified for the sins of those who believe and have faith in Him. Unfortunately, the non-Christian tries for a repeat performance every time something happens where religion is involved and is at the forefront in yelling "crucify him".'

'God has given us a free will, and these men have misused the freedom given to them in that they have molested children rather than follow God's teachings. They have, in fact, given up their Christian beliefs and, while still wearing the robes, have kneeled before Lucifer and have agreed to declare him king by becoming sexual predators. God will judge them for what they have done, and their punishment will be more than appropriate to the crime they have inflicted on these children and the fraud perpetrated in the church's name. In these instances,

Christians should not abandon their beliefs and have faith and should pray for the victims.'

'Unfortunately, the non-Christians will blame religion and not the person, as this generally fits their agenda. If a doctor malpractices, we do not lay the claim against all doctors in the country or the medical body or association. Just that doctor. Unfortunately, they do not apply the same principle to religion, even though it is a single minister who has done the act and not God. The minister has a free choice whether he acts according to the Christian beliefs or what the devil is telling him to do, and in these cases, they follow the devil and abandon their beliefs.'

'To those who are victims of pedophilia and other abhorred acts, I would urge you to seek the Lord's help and leave the retribution to Him. This is hard but the only way for the true Christian. The debate regarding compensation is tricky as those who have suffered at the hands of the perpetrators have had to deal with various mental issues which would have prevented them from earning an income or a higher income. Yet some consider compensation to be a worldly response to these appalling acts and not a Christian response.'

'Those affected who pursue compensation have adopted the way of this world and not the teachings of the Lord, as if money will compensate them for the horror inflicted on them. Most times, they have abandoned their faith entirely and have knelt before Lucifer and adopt the way of the world and demand compensation. According to them, God and society have let them down. To those who think this way, I can only say that God has not abandoned you and would therefore ask that you seek His help in finding peace and a resolution to the suffering and pain that has been inflicted on you. God will hear your prayers and will deal with the matter the way He deems fit and at the time of His choosing. Your compensation is in the next life, not in this one, and will be a permanent compensation and not temporary. Seek the Lord's help and have faith.'

'Many in the congregation feel that an ordained minister is something special as an agent of God or one of His prophets. This is not the case, and if anyone tells you otherwise, they are lying. Ministers are in churches to spread the Word of God. You can do it. The only difference is that you may not be trained as to what the Bible says, and you may mislead other parishioners because your interpretation is wrong.'

'When you pray, you do not pray to the minister or a saint or Mary and ask them to deliver your message via Express Post to Jesus Christ, care of the Kingdom of Heaven. You pray direct to the man himself, Jesus. When God responds to your prayer, He does so directly to you and not through a minister or other means.'

'So, your relationship and faith are directly with and in God and not indirectly through another body, person, or medium. You should pray directly to God, frequently and respectfully.'

'Let us pray...'

Chapter 19

After the mass, Simon stood at the entrance of the church, saying goodbye to the congregation when he was approached by Emily and Stephen. They introduced themselves and asked if they could speak to Simon in private.

Simon led them to a room in the hall and said, 'What seems to be the problem?'

Emily said, 'We want to get married. We came from a community some three hours' drive from here but had to leave as my father would not allow us to marry. He wants me to marry a professional man. Stephen and I have known each other since we were in primary school and have always been together. My mother does not want to start trouble, so she doesn't say anything but just follows what my father says. We have tried to reason with my father, but he won't listen and will not allow us to get on with our lives. We are both 23 years of age and both have jobs. Stephen works as a plumber, and I work as a sales assistant in town. We have rented a house locally, and both have been brought up in the Christian faith.'

'At 23, you may decide for yourself what you want to do. But whatever you do, try to prevent a split-up with your parents. Will it help if I ring your father and have a word with him?'

'I doubt it. The last time we were at home, Stephen called in, and we both approached my father to see if he would be reasonable, but he wouldn't even consider us getting married.'

Stephen said, 'I always refer to Em's father as Sunshine, as he is the opposite. He basically told me never to come around, and if I did, he would shoot me. He told Em to go up to her room and stay there. She is 23 years of age and can't decide for herself. It was on that day that we decided to get out and make a start on our own. The next day, Em's father had to go interstate on business. We packed whatever belongings we were going to take and drove off. Em's mother gave us a big kiss and hug and wished us both well. My parents always supported us getting married and gave us some money to carry us over. We consider ourselves Christians and want to know what we can do as we want to have a family.'

Simon said, 'Well, as Christians, you should follow God's Word, and I would recommend you ask the good Lord for guidance and His blessing.'

'We've done that. I saw our minister, Peter Sutherland, who told us it was all right to live together unmarried as a good percentage of people do it these days. It is the way the world is heading. However, Em was convinced that was not right and checked the Bible and found it said the opposite. It said sex was not to be partaken outside of marriage.'

'That's correct. The Bible warns of marrying a non-Christian, and sex can only be partaken of a marriage. To do otherwise is to commit adultery. The rules are not to stop you from enjoying what God gave to Adam and Eve, but to protect the sanctity of marriage and abide by the commandments given to Moses.'

Emily asked, 'What do we do?'

Simon replied, 'First, you cannot get married without applying and waiting thirty-one days. You will have to go and apply at the town hall tomorrow. We will book you in for a private wedding on a Tuesday in thirty-two days' time. We will have a small group here on that day that can bear witness, and my wife will help with the ceremony. I will need your birth certificates so I can register you after the marriage ceremony.'

Stephen said, 'I will tell my parents. They will definitely come.'

Simon added, 'In the meantime, Emily, I will make arrangements for you to stay at Mrs. Jones's house until you're married. I know she has a spare room and will be more than happy for you to stay with her. We most probably will use her as a witness. What are your contact details? Can you please jot those down for me and fill out these forms and drop them back to me within a week?'

They shook hands, and the party split up, making their way to their cars and home. Stephen, upon arriving home, called his mother, and both his father and mother were thrilled to hear about the wedding and agreed to be there on that day. Emily sent an SMS to her mother and asked her to ring her when she was able. She did this two days later.

Emily said, 'Hi, Mum. Thanks for ringing. Well, we have arranged to be married in a month's time. Mum, Mum, why are you crying?'

Her mother said, 'Because I can't – she sobbed – 'see my daughter get married,' and burst into tears. 'It would create a big argument if I came, and your father would never forgive me.' Again, she burst into tears.

Emily said, 'Mum, you're upset, so I better let you go. Love you. Bye.' Emily went home with a heavy heart and upset.

Chapter 20

Peter, minister at St Andrews, stood and entered the pulpit. 'This Sunday, I have been asked to cover who or what is God as I understand some of you are having trouble with the concept of God and how He fits into your life. We will not be answering the technical points as to the properties of God as most understand this, and the understanding that you require is not a technical one but rather a practical layperson's understanding of this concept and where He fits into your life.'

'According to the Bible, God is the Creator of heaven and earth. Scientists dispute this and have raised several theories which most of us have accepted as being relevant, and their version probably happened. We are told God created the heaven and earth in seven days. These days, most people do not believe this and believe the earth was created over many thousands of years and not seven days. So do we have a God who lies to us or exaggerates the truth? Scientists think we do.'

'We read in the Bible about Job and that the Lord allowed all his family to be killed by Lucifer and all of Job's wealth taken from him for no other reason than to show how righteous Job was. The Bible tells us in Exodus that the Lord inflicted ten curses on the pharaoh to prove to the other gods who were the most powerful one of them. The same God destroyed half of those whom He led out of Egypt because they took up idolatry as a golden calf. The other half were not allowed into the Promised Land because they feared the occupants who were described as giants would annihilate them. They were made to walk for forty years in the desert until they died, and their descendants found favor with the Lord. The God that you read about in the Bible is a God whom many ministers will have you believe is an all-loving, compassionate God, but the Bible tells a different story. Who is the God whom we say you should have faith in? This is the question that you should answer yourself.'

'When you become a Christian, you go through trials to enable yourself to get to trust Jesus and understand the meaning of faith. Many are tested in an area that they never thought the Lord would go. Some have lost loved ones for no reason at all and are left on their own without companions or support. They pray to God for an understanding of why this has happened, but get no response. They sense God has left them, for there is this constant emptiness and loneliness, and this is not just momentarily. It goes on for weeks, months, and could go on for years. They despair and believe that God has left them, and they drift away from God as what He has preached and taught them in practice in relation to love and faith has not been their experience.'

'So your understanding of God will, in reality, be the circumstances you find yourself in and the reaction or response you are getting to your prayers. Each must make their own judgement, but what many have told me is that they have not moved away from Jesus, but rather, they feel He has left them. They view this as God saying, "You are unworthy of my presence, and you continue to sin. Therefore, you deserve no support from me. I, God, consider you a lost cause." While I concur with what you are saying, I can only urge you to seek God out and ask Him to show you the way. If you receive no response, then you have to make the best judgement you can and do your best in the circumstances. I would urge you not to give up coming to church. Heaven only knows we need your weekly contributions. No, I shouldn't say that, as some may take me seriously and not as a joke. You must decide and find a compromise that suits your style of living. If God feels you are doing something sinful or contrary to his plan, He will let you know. Remember what happened to Jonah? He ended up in a whale's stomach and put back on course. So will you.'

'A rich man approached Jesus and said, "Teacher, tell me what I must do to get eternal life." Jesus replied, "Sell everything you possess and give it to the poor and follow me." If I told you to do this, would you? You will look at your watch and say, "Thank God we only have another fifteen minutes to go before we break up." There is no way that any of you would do this. To live in this world takes an effort, and no one gives you a thing. You did not ask to be put on this earth. You were born and started with nothing, and by your struggles and effort, you try to put a roof over your family's head. You try to educate your children and set them up for their lives ahead. No one gives you a thing along the way. Nor is there any help. In fact, it is a battle to keep your head above water and to meet the continuously mounting bills. Your prayers are never answered, and at the end of the week, you seem to go backwards, not being able to put away anything for that stormy day that you know will whip the feet from under you. Yet we are told, "Sell everything and follow me."

'Really? How many would do this? You go to your wife and to your children who are of school age and say, "Guess what – I am going to sell the house and give it to the poor, and we are going to live off charity and under a bench in the park." What do you think would be their reaction? I put it to you that your decision must be made in a context of what you want to do with your life. It is said that this approach is contrary to the teachings of the Bible, as you are basically saying to God,

"I believe this is the plan, and please help me achieve it. Otherwise, I will do it on my own."

'I disagree as first, you have a plan which, in most cases, God doesn't, or if He does, you don't get to know about it. Second, you put your effort into achieving the plan, which helps your family and the community. It helps the church as you pay tithes. It helps the state as you pay taxes. The worst thing is not to have any relationship with God at all. The next would be to have an infrequent relationship – namely, God is considered at times of emergencies, and then according to you, He does not perform to your demands, and therefore, there is no God. You must have a relationship with God, and it should be actively pursued.'

'Let's bow our heads and pray...'

Chapter 21

Simon was at work on the commencement of a new week. Close to the end of his shift, he was loading a truck and noticed the driver in a subdued manner.

He said, 'What's up, mate? You seem worried.'

The driver said, 'My father is in hospital and is dying of cancer and has only a few days left.'

'Is he a Christian?'

'Ah... He believes in God. I think he does. He swears enough in the name of Jesus Christ.'

'Would you like me to see him with you?'

'Yes, you can go after you finish loading me, and I can meet you there.'

'Well, I didn't mean this minute.'

'He could be dead if we waited.'

'All right. My shift ends in half an hour, and I will meet you there. What's his name, and which hospital is he at?'

'I will write it down for you.'

Simon finished his shift, washed his hands, collected his lunchbox, went to his car, and drove off. He pulled into the hospital car park and saw the name Calvary on the front of the hospital.

He went into the hospital and asked the receptionist at the desk how he would get to the room written on his note. The receptionist gave him directions, and off Simon went. He walked down the long hospital hallway till he reached room 821 and entered a room which had four beds in it, but only one was being occupied. He went up to the person and noted the truck driver standing next to the man and assumed this was his father.

Simon put out his hand and said, 'Mr. Richards, I believe.'

Richards said, 'Yes. My son was telling me he asked you to come. I am sorry you have wasted your time. I don't need someone telling me about religious rubbish. I know where I am headed, and it's south.'

'Why? Because you don't believe in Jesus Christ? What, you have no faith in him?'

'I have lived a life that I am not proud of, and no one will forgive me. I have killed a man and, in my younger days, even robbed a few service stations and snatched a few bags from rich chicks who think they are above the rest of us.'

'You know, when Jesus Christ was crucified, the good Lord made sure He was with company and not on His own. It wasn't an isolated event. It reflected the community at large. You had the lawmakers present – the Pharisees. You had the police there – the Romans. There were onlookers who previously were screaming, "Crucify Him!" You had Mary Magdalene and Mary the mother of Jesus and his brother James there, seeing him being put to death. To the right of him was a man sentenced to be crucified, and he acknowledged he deserved to be there. He also acknowledged that Christ was innocent and should not be there. However, he did not know the purpose as to why an innocent man was put to death and why there were two guilty criminals on either side of him. He did not know that it was God Himself who put Jesus there, so mankind could decide whether they wanted eternal life or the termination of life at death. They also did not know that Jesus so loved mankind, that He was willing to give up His life so His creation could have eternal life if they had faith in Him. There were two sinful men and one good guy there. The criminal on his right said, "Lord, remember me when you go to heaven." Jesus said, "Truly, I say unto you that from this day, you will be in heaven with me in paradise." He forgave whatever the person had done on this earth because the criminal had faith in Jesus to be the true God. His sins were wiped that minute and would be taken to the cross by Jesus. The cross is what you should concentrate on, and you should say to Jesus, "I have made a mess of my life, the one you gave me. Please forgive me for my sins in your name, as only you can do this." None of your sins is bad enough to prevent Jesus from forgiving you and giving you eternal life. Ask for it and believe and have faith in Him.'

'I thank you for coming and will think about what you have said.'

Simon got up, shook Mr. Richards's hand, left, leaving the two to chat, walked to his car, and drove home.

Two days later, Simon saw the driver at one of the loading docks and yelled out, 'How's your father?'

The driver walked up to Simon and said, 'You certainly made an impression on him. He kept talking about what you had said. I left an hour later, and he was still taking to himself about his sins and Jesus. The next morning, we received a phone call from Calvary, where my father was staying. He died in the early hours of the morning. They said that normally, he was restless in his sleep, but that night, he slept quietly and died with a smile on his face.'

'Sorry to hear he had died.'

'Thanks for all you did for him. I believe he made peace with God before he died. It looks like he carried that burden all his life.'

Both shook hands, and Simon went off to load another truck. Simon sat on his forklift and thanked God for taking care of Mr. Richards and his soul.

Chapter 22

Simon had finished his day's work and made his way to clock off. He grabbed his time card, inserted it in the machine, and clocked off. He went to his car and drove out of the car park and onto the street to go home. He was coming up to a small shopping centre when he noticed a person lying on the ground, facing the brick wall at the entrance. There were drivers moving in and out of the shopping center's car park, and no one stopped. Also, there was a bus stop nearby, and people were waiting for their bus, but no one was around the person. Simon parked his car in the shopping centre and walked over to the body lying against the wall.

He said, 'Hello, are you all right?'

There was no response. There were people at the bus stop, but no one came over to enquire about the person or what Simon was doing. Simon leaned over the person and shook the body. There was no response. He leaned over the person and saw that he was breathing, but with some difficulty. Simon straightened up, grabbed his mobile phone out of his pocket, dialed emergency services, and asked for an ambulance.

The operator asked, 'Is the person still breathing?'

Simon answered, 'Yes, but very shallow. He seems to have difficulty. Should I roll him over or sit him up?'

'Are you able to sit him up so he can breathe without weight on his chest?'

'I will sit him up and see.'

Simon picked the man up, set him up against the brick wall, and saw if there were any indications of improvement. 'He is sitting up at present and seems to breathe better. The ambulance has arrived. I will leave it to them to handle him. Thanks for your help.'

The ambulance arrived within minutes, and the paramedics quickly worked on the man. They gave the man some oxygen and took his blood pressure and said it was low. He had a heart attack, and they rushed him to the hospital. They put him on a stretcher and into the ambulance. They closed the rear door and drove off with the siren blaring.

Simon went to his car and drove home. He told Monique, who wasn't surprised that no one had come to the stranger's help.

Monique said, 'These days, people look after themselves and don't care about others. The poor person could have died there, and no one would care. Thank God you were able to spot him and lend a hand. Did he seem to be a local?'

Simon said, 'I don't know. I didn't get a chance to see if he had any ID on him. He didn't have an alert around his neck or on his wrist. He was dressed in casual wear and seemed an average bloke.'

'I hope he is all right and the good Lord watches over him. I have prayed for him.'

Chapter 23

Simon was at work and was approached by the operations manager, who introduced himself as Frank Butterworth.

Frank said, 'I am in a spot of bother in that I have to present a speaker tomorrow to a business lunch at the Journalist Club. There will be about 150 members attending. My guest speaker has taken ill and is in hospital with a busted appendix. I wondered if you would attend in his place.'

Simon said, 'You must be desperate, asking a forklift driver.'

'I am desperate, but I understand you are a minister of the local church, and we never had a minister or anyone talking about religion at our gatherings. I thought it would help members to hear what the church thinks of commerce and profitability. Money issues. I will leave it up to yourself to decide what topic you want to speak about.'

'I will need time off to prepare.'

'Take tomorrow morning off and meet me here, say, at twelve, and we will drive in together.'

'Good with me.'

Simon didn't have a clue what he would say to the meeting, but he knew it had to be good, as it was critical to leave them with a message that God loved them. He went back to work and begun loading another truck.

The next morning, Simon got up early and prayed for wisdom and that he wouldn't make a fool of himself. He sat down in front of his computer and typed. He worked away, looked up, and noticed the time – eleven thirty. He quickly grabbed his papers, put them in his bag, and went to the bathroom to shower. He came out, got dressed in a suit and tie, picked up his briefcase, went to his car, and drove off to work. At work, he parked his car and walked to the operations manager's office. He knocked on the door and entered.

Frank said, 'I was fearing you wouldn't turn up.'

Simon said, 'No, I'm here. I will do my best to get the message across.'

'We better be off. Otherwise, we will be late.'

Both men walked out of the building, got into Frank's car, and drove to the club. Parking was at a premium, so they had to park in one of the reserved spots and walk to the club.

They went through the front door, and Simon was introduced to the club manager, who took him into a large room where people were settled and others were coming in. Simon was shown the speaker's stand and was given a glass of water. They waited for about fifteen minutes. Then after, everyone was seated.

Lunch was served. Simon looked around and thought, *Thank God I am speaking after lunch and not before.* They would have had a few drinks and may not be as aggressive towards him. He then thought, *Why I am worried? God will not let me make a fool of myself. I am not a poor speaker. I am not Moses. Could be Aaron.* They gave Simon a plate but refused to have dinner, saying he had already eaten. He refused wine but accepted a glass of water and went over his notes.

After everyone had finished and the plates were cleared, the club manager stood and said, 'Ladies and gentlemen. Our speaker for today is a minister of the local church and will be speaking on the topic "Business Profiting by Religion". His name is Simon Fuller, and I would appreciate you giving him a warm welcome.'

Simon stood up as the meeting attendees applauded and moved to the speaker's stand, pausing while looking at the audience.

Simon began, 'Thank you for a warm welcome. I recognize some of you who are part of my congregation. It must be the reason why I haven't been thrown to the lions as entertainment as yet. Isn't that what normally happens to a Christian?'

The crowd laughed, and Simon settled in.

'With it being lunchtime, we will pass the plate around shortly. I hope you will be generous.'

The meeting burst into laughter and then applause.

'When religion is spoken about in businesses, it is whispered and not spoken out loud. The reason is quite simple. It is because most businesspeople prefer not to involve themselves with religion and concentrate on the money aspects of business, as they feel there is a conflict there. The problem here is not so much in making profits but how it is made and its distribution.'

'When Jesus Christ was around, most of the larger centers were very prosperous, and there were a lot of wealthy people about at that time. It was quite normal for Jesus to be invited to a wealthy person's house to dine, and he never spoke contrary to doing business or making a profit. Yes, he overturned the tables at the synagogue of the money merchants, but that is a story which must be left for another time.'

'The thing I want to talk about is, can you be a Christian and still be in business? The good Lord said to a wealthy man, "If you want to follow me, sell all that you have and give it to the poor." The man unfortunately misunderstood the message, thinking he had to reduce himself to beggar status before he could get eternal life. This is not the case, and what was being said to him was because all that he had lived for were his possessions and money, the tangible things of life that, for him, in his circumstances, if he wanted eternal life, he should sell and give to the poor.

'The Bible refers to profits and business throughout both the Old Testament and the New Testament and lays a plan what is ethical and what is not in relation to business, the earning of profits, and the distribution of wealth. The Bible makes it clear why you are on this earth, and that is to serve God. It doesn't mean you cannot apply your great skill to earn profits. It really means that your skills have to achieve more of an outcome and be distributed more fairly amongst the community and the genuine poor. You were put on the earth to serve God and not your employer or another substitute god, such as money, power, and greed.'

'I have seen situations where luck has played a great degree in a business's success, and yet the same principles have been applied by others who have found themselves in an opposite situation. The businessman has never questioned these opportunities and grabs them when they come without thought or concern about why they arose. Why do they come? Well, not because of the great skill of the entrepreneur or businessperson. No, it is the Lucifer element that causes it, and they give no consideration as to the consequences of selling one's soul when this happens. The only payment that needs to be made is to kneel before Lucifer and declare him king of this world and he will ensure you get what you desire to secure your allegiance to him.'

'Jesus was confronted in the wilderness with such a proposition, as you will be. He refused to accept it as His father will give Him far more than what was being offered now. A prize that cannot be taken from

Him in the future and one that is vastly more than what was being offered by Lucifer. When you are confronted with these opportunities out of the blue, you too should consider whether the offer is worth the risk because to give away your eternal life and all that God has offered you for a short quick profit or benefit is a very high price to pay.'

'I want today to lecture not on the areas briefly touched upon but on you as an individual, for we hear many instances when businesspeople have nervous and marriage breakdowns and commit suicide, and the list goes on only because they are alone or the god that they relied on or trusted namely Lucifer or themselves, has let them down. Most businesspeople whom I know work hard at their job and, unfortunately, too hard as they believe there is no choice. You either work yourself into the ground or get replaced. The god that is to provide them with success is them. They have no time for family or church but only the hard grind, as this is the only thing that brings in the money. Some, unfortunately, see the family as on the other side of the ledger who take the money out, which often leads to a breakdown and separation. Money is the only thing in life.'

'This polarized executive never considers Christianity as it conflicts with his principles of stopping at nothing to achieve his goal of maximizing profitability, getting his way. He never stops to consider, "Why am I doing this? What's the purpose of my life, and is this what God wants me to do, for it is He who put me on this earth?" Most executives I have met who have been in their jobs for several years get to hate their job, and it affects them mentally and physically. It is what they wanted at the beginning, and yes, it produces goods and chattels but gives them no joy, and it is exactly what they will do for the rest of their lives right here and in hell.'

'You see, unless you take a grip on yourself, you will never try to find out what God meant you to be. He may have a plan that you will be chairman of the board while you're stuck in an office tallying up figures. You have become what you have connived and not allowed God, who created you, to tell you what plan He has in line for you. Basically, you have taken control of your own life and, as a result, have achieved far less than He had planned for you. You could be feeling the pressure, and your family may suffer because of this. You could become aggressive towards your wife and children and do something that you will regret later.'

'I often ask businesspeople if they have a needle. A sewing needle. Most say no. "Why do you want it?" I tell them it is the first requirement to see if they have eternal life. They always ask, "And what is the second?" A camel. You see, it would be easier to push a camel through a needle than to get someone who is relying on themselves to say, "I have failed. Now let's give it over to Jesus Christ and see what He can do with my life."

'So I urge you to consider your position and ask yourself whether it is all that you thought it would be or if you believe you can do better. Is there more to life than what you, on your own, have achieved? Is your family suffering from the polarization of your life? If you believe they are, then ask Jesus Christ, and He will show you how you can go about achieving what He had planned for you, or come and see me, and both of us will ask for His help in prayer.'

'Remember, to do nothing is to wait for death, and then it is too late to change course. If you do not have faith, you will stay chipping at the pile of rocks and getting nowhere. You can accumulate a fortune on this earth and still be the most miserable person on this earth, and you will not take it with you.'

'Thank you for listening to me.'

There was applause.

The club manager asked, 'Has anyone any questions?'

One hand was raised. A man in a very expensive suit got up and said, 'I understand Peter Sutherland from St Andrews Church has said for those who lack faith, they may gain internal life through good deeds and encouraged us to donate to the various projects at his church. What do you say about getting eternal life through good deeds?'

Simon replied, 'Sir, I put you down as a wise Pharisee, for you know the answer but still tempt the Word of God. Good deeds are part of the commandments relating to "Love thy neighbor". Help your fellow man, those in genuine need or who have had some misfortune. But if you want eternal life, then there is only one way, and that is to believe in Jesus Christ and have faith in Him. Remember, even Jesus said, "There will come many in my name, but most are against me," and therefore, I urge you to stop trying to find the shortcut but go to Jesus and beg forgiveness and ask Him for His help. You will then be on the road to eternal life. Are there any more questions? No. Then thank you for having me?'

There was applause. Simon moved to go out of the club.

Chapter 24

One Saturday a few weeks later, in the evening, both Simon and Monique were sitting on their couch, watching a movie on TV, when there was a knock at the front door.

Simon got up and opened the door and said, 'Can I help you?'

There was a middle-aged man of good appearance on the other side who said, 'Hello, my name is Robert Burton. I am the minister at St Andrews Church, close to here. I believe I owe you a debt of gratitude for saving my life. I came to say thanks.'

Simon remembered the person. Even though he looked different now, he could still see it was the same man whom he had helped some weeks ago at the shopping centre. He put out his hand and said, 'Nice to meet you. Please come inside.'

They walked to their lounge, where Monique was still sitting, watching the movie on TV.

Simon said, 'Darling, this is Mr. Burton, the minister of St Andrews Church. He was the man I had found on the footpath some weeks ago and called an ambulance to assist.'

Monique got up and said, 'Nice to meet you. I am Monique. Please sit down.' Monique picked up the control and switched the TV off.

Simon asked, 'Can I get you a drink or a cup of coffee?'

Robert said, 'No, thank you. I don't want to disrupt your evening. All I wanted to do is to come and say thank you for helping me when I collapsed some weeks ago. The good Lord always said, "Love thy neighbor," and you have certainly shown you follow His Word. Do you go to church? If you don't, I would welcome you to mine.'

'Thanks, but I have my own church. Small, but it keeps me busy providing services on Sunday and working in a factory the other five days a week to earn a living.'

'Oh, you're a minister of religion as well. Sorry. I did not know. Why are you working in a factory when you could look after a congregation?'

'It is a long story.'

'Please tell me. I am interested to hear what has happened.'

Simon told Mr. Robert what had happened and why he found himself out of a job.

Robert said, 'I also received the same letter from the archdeacon but continued to be God centered by preaching. I guess they haven't caught up with me yet, or I am too small for them to worry about me. But they are definitely chasing the money. I am due to move up to a senior position next week. Possibly, this will be when the problem will come to a head.'

Simon said, 'I hope all goes well for you. Keep me informed about how you get on.'

Both got up and shook hands, and Simon walked Mr. Robert out to the front door.

Chapter 25

The month seemed to have flown by, and the day arrived for Emily and Stephen's wedding. Stephen's parents were in town and would attend the wedding. Emily borrowed a wedding dress that Mrs. Jones had put away, and all the formalities had been attended to except the pinning up of the dress to make sure it fit perfectly on Emily.

Mrs. Jones said, 'Now, Em, stand still so I can pin the dress on you. It seems we will have to take it up a bit and in. I'll just go out and get my pins.'

Emily looked in the mirror and saw the dress needed to be pinned in and taken up, but looked gorgeous, and she was smiling from ear to ear. Mrs. Jones returned with a small box containing pins and started to fit the dress around Emily when there was a knock at the front door. She went to the door, and it was her friend Betty from down the street.

Betty said, 'Just thought I would pop in to see if you needed a hand with anything.'

Mrs. Jones said, 'Not at this minute, but you can come in and have a chat while I fix the wedding dress.'

Both ladies went in to where Emily was standing, and Betty introduced herself. 'Hello. You must be Emily. You certainly look stunning in that dress. Let me give you a hand in pinning it up.'

Mrs. Jones said, 'That would be helpful.'

Both ladies got to work when there was another knock at the door. Betty went and open the door and recognized her neighbours and invited them in.

Mrs. Jones said, 'Girls, nice to see you. Have you come for a chit-chat, or do you want to help?' She then noticed each of the ladies had a bottle of champagne in each hand. 'Now, what do you intend to do with that? Is it for the wedding?'

A neighbor explained, 'Well, originally, we brought them for the wedding, but I guess it won't hurt us to have a drink to help calm Emily's nerves and to give her a bit of a send-off. You know, her last day as a single girl, a miss.'

A bottle of champagne was opened, and Betty rushed to find five glasses. She came in with an assortment of glasses, and the champagne was tipped in the glass and the bottle emptied.

Mrs. Jones said, 'Well, Emily, you look stunning. Take a big drink to steady your nerves. Girls. To Emily.'

Everyone raised her glass and took a big drink, with Mrs. Jones and Betty both emptying their glasses.

Betty said, 'Now that was nice. We better get to work.'

All four ladies pin Emily up when there was a further knock at the door. One neighbor went to the door and brought back four other ladies, each carrying trays of food.

Betty said, 'You can put the food on the kitchen table, girls. The perishables can go into the fridge. What do you reckon, girls?'

Everyone exclaimed, 'She looks beautiful!'

One girl who had brought some of the food said, 'I see you got champagne. We should have a drink for Emily. A bit of a girl's send-off. This being her last day as a miss.'

One of them grabbed a bottle of champagne and filled the glasses that were there when another one lady went to the kitchen cupboard and brought back some glasses which were abruptly filled. Another bottle of champagne was used to top these glasses up, and all ladies raised their glasses and yelled out. 'To Emily!' and down went the champagne.

Betty and Mrs. Jones helped Emily take her dress off and slip into a robe and then sewed up the hem and the other parts of the dress.

One girl yelled out, 'You only have one bottle of champagne left! I'll go home and see what I have at home.'

The others all darted out of the house and, within fifteen minutes, returned with an assortment of wine and spirits.

Mrs. Jones said, 'Help yourself, girls.'

Each of the ladies went to fill her glass and told stories of what happened on her wedding day.

They sat there till lunchtime, talking, when one lady yelled out, 'Is there anything to eat?'

Mrs. Jones answered, 'Not really. I didn't expect so many of you to turn up, so I didn't prepare anything.'

One girl said, 'Don't worry. We can have the sandwiches out of the tray we brought over. There's plenty.'

The girls all got stuck in the food and drink, still talking about their weddings and husbands, and letting him wait at the church, etc. They all had advice about what to do and not to do on the night after the service and when you were alone with your husband. All had stories to tell, and those who didn't have one recalled what a star had done on her wedding night, as shown on Netflix or some other show.

By four o'clock, most were well over their limits and had eaten all the sandwiches that they had brought in. Some were even slurring their words, while others lay down on the floor and went to sleep. Most couldn't walk to the bathroom without falling over and bursting into laughter. Mrs. Jones and Betty had finished sewing up the dress. However, Emily had also consumed a bit of drink and was feeling under the weather. She lay on the lounge and fell asleep.

Emily woke up after sleeping for an hour and said, 'Oh my god, it's five thirty, and I have to get to the church to get married!'

Emily hurried to the shower and had a shower and did her face and hair as best she could. There was a knock at the front door, and she went to open it. It was her brother, Ben.

Ben asked, 'Well, Em, are you ready?'

Emily answered, 'Not quite. There is going to be a bit of a wait. Ben, you look nice in your suit. Sit on the veranda while I slip into my wedding dress.'

Emily went back into the house and tried to wake up Mrs. Jones and Betty, but neither of them would wake up. Both were snoring their heads off. She decided not to persist but get dressed and get to the hall where Stephen would be waiting. Emily slipped into her wedding dress, touched up her make-up, put on her shoes, and rushed out of the house, leaving the ladies to sleep off their celebration.

Six thirty arrived, and everyone was in the hall, waiting for the bride, who should have been there at six o'clock. Stephen waited impatiently, wondering about the delay or whether Em's father made an appearance. The music started up, and her brother Ben led Emily down the aisle.

Unfortunately, Emily had grabbed someone else's shoes and not her own. These were slightly wider than hers and had heels a couple of inches higher. She walked down the aisle but couldn't walk straight, and Stephen was looking at her, moving up and down, left and right, not being able to keep her balance. She tried to hang onto Ben's arm but still walked as if she was blind drunk. Emily finally got to the front of the church, and the ceremony began.

Stephen and Emily exchanged their vows and were pronounced man and wife by Simon. Stephen and Emily kissed each other, and the guests swelled around to shake Stephen's hand and to kiss Emily and congratulate both of them. Emily took off her shoes and handed them to Ben. The rest she was going to do barefoot.

Simon and Monique had arranged a small smorgasbord as there appeared to be no function arranged. Everyone grabbed a sandwich and a Coke and afterwards wished the couple well. The wedding broke up at eight, as everyone had to go to work the next morning. Stephen took Emily's bags out of Ben's car and put them in his. Emily and Stephen drove off, followed by the other members of the party. They drove home to their rented house, which had been occupied by Stephen for the last month.

Stephen took Emily's bags into their bedroom and went to the kitchen to get a soft drink. He sat in the kitchen, thinking, *well, I am a married man, but what do I do now?* He sipped his soft drink to give Emily enough time to prepare herself for the consummation ceremony – whatever that was.

He sat there for about half an hour and couldn't hear any noise coming from the bedroom. He got up and walked into the bedroom and saw Emily lying on the bed in her underwear, sound asleep. He covered her with a blanket and picked up her wedding dress off the floor and put it on a chair. He went back into the kitchen and got a beer, knowing that there would be no sex that night. He made a bed for himself on the lounge and drank his beer and went to bed.

The next morning, Stephen got up and headed off to work, leaving Emily still in bed. Emily woke up at about ten in the morning and stumbled out of bed. She saw her wedding dress on the chair and realized what had happened. Partying with the girls was too much for Emily, who was not a drinker. Around midday, Mrs. Jones came over and apologized, and was deeply upset that she had missed the wedding.

About four o'clock, Stephen arrived home, not sure what to expect, possibly another pizza for dinner. Emily greeted him at the door with a kiss, and both went to the bedroom, where Stephen took his work clothes off and then went to have a shower. When he came out of the shower, Emily was in bed, waiting for him, and they consummated the marriage.

Stephen couldn't stop laughing after Emily told him what had happened on the wedding day, why she had fallen asleep, about the shoes, and her walk down the aisle.

Chapter 26

The archdeacon visited Peter Sutherland's office, unexpected and unannounced. He wanted to advise Peter that shortly, one of his senior ministers would resign, and there would be a position to be filled by someone he could rely on. Peter reminded the archdeacon of the help he had given financially towards the refurbishing works of the archdeacon's church and towards the construction of several new buildings and offices.

The archdeacon acknowledged Peter's dedication and help and got up and moved to the back of Peter's chair. He stroked Peter's shoulders and kiss him on the back of the neck and run his hands down Peter's chest. He then unbuttoned Peter's shirt and unzip his pants and stroked Peter's penis.

Peter was first surprised but then got up, and both men undressed, and Peter got on the couch, followed by the archdeacon. Both men embraced and prepared to position themselves for a homosexual encounter.

Suddenly, the door was flung open, and Peter's secretary was standing in the doorway with Peter's wife. Both stared at what they saw with their mouths open, speechless for a minute, and then turned quickly and ran out of the office, leaving the door wide open.

Peter got dressed and ran after his secretary. He abused her for coming in but then realized he needs her support and calmed down. Peter told his secretary she should forget what she saw, or she would lose her job, and any reference would describe her as a liar and an untrustworthy person.

Peter arrived home to confront his wife and tell her what had happened, that if they wanted to get the new position and advance in the world, they would have to provide the archdeacon with what he wanted. Both agreed that it would be a small price to pay for a big gain, one that would normally not present itself again soon. Who knows? Someday he may also become the replacement for the archdeacon.

The sight of Peter with another man had made a lasting impression on his wife, who moved out of the main bedroom and from then on slept in the spare room. She refused to have sex with her husband, which caused tension between them, and often arguments arose over the subject.

Peter frequented several brothels to get sex, which was no longer being provided by his wife.

Chapter 27

It was Sunday, and Peter was before his congregation in the pulpit at St Andrews church.

Peter said, 'The week seems to fly by quickly these days. Today I would like to raise several issues which have been raised with me during the week and seem to be a concern to several members of the congregation.'

'First, the matter of divorce. The Bible allows divorce only in a number of circumstances, infidelity being the main one. But this was unreasonable, and even in Moses's days, people would seek the right to divorce when the marriage had broken down for a multitude of reasons, and Moses granted these in certain cases when there were irreconcilable differences.'

'Today the church tries to stick to the Bible's teachings but, in reality, finds this impossible as incompatibility and not willing to see the marriage through are the main reasons causing divorces. A very large percentage of the population divorce, whether or not the church likes it, and if it is done with the blessing of the scriptures, then good. Otherwise, who cares as we don't care as we are divorcing irrespectively? Family law has become a big industry, and many a billionaire has lost much of their wealth divorcing several times.'

'It is unfortunate that these days, most people do not stay together to give their marriage a real go, but rather dip their toe in the water and then declare it is not for them. Most have lived in a de facto relationship before marrying, which in itself is not contrary to the teachings of the Bible. It is the aspect of having sex while unmarried that is the sinful act here.'

'These days, we also have same-sex marriages, which are contrary to the teachings of the Bible but are in line with the laws of the State. The church is trying to come to terms with this, and at present, the position is that the church will not marry a same-sex couple as it still does not recognize this to be a marriage but rather a relationship. The church will allow a divorce when there is harm inflicted on one partner by the other. I say it in this way as some women are bigger and more powerful than the men they marry. The church tries to accommodate divorces, and most times, tries to give counselling. However, many ministers will not bother as they feel members of their congregation will do what they want to do anyway, so why give advice?'

'Second, on the matter of homosexuality, this is not a new thing. The Bible covers it in a contradictory way because it says it should never be allowed to exist, yet it says we should love our neighbor. This matter is still being developed, but it is clear to most churches that any sinner is always welcomed in a church and allowed to seek God. It is the homosexual act that the church objects to. Any two same-sex individuals can live together. It is the act that the church objects to. Our church says that we welcome all sinners, and we are not here to judge but rather help whenever called upon.'

'The third point that I wish to raise also refers to last week's sermon. Remember, it was about God. The question is that if I am getting nowhere with my prayers, should I take the initiative and start deciding for myself? In doing this, am I becoming idolatrous? My initial response would be to say yes as you are saying, "I know better than God." But in thinking about it, you are not saying that at all. What you are saying is, "If there is no communication between God and myself, then I have no alternative but to decide. Otherwise, the bus will run over me, or I will do something about it". Then, if this is the case, the answer is no. You are not substituting yourself for God. It is just God who chooses not to communicate with you. You try to do your best until He comes around. You basically must decide what's good for you while upholding your beliefs and ensuring you don't break any laws of the land.'

'Let us pray...'

Chapter 28

The archdeacon called in at Peter's office to inform him of his promotion. His wife was there, and she was very pleased and excited. They decided to go to dinner to celebrate. Peter decided to drive, and they all got into his white BMW and headed down the highway. They called into a wine bar first and ordered champagne and toasted one another's success.

The archdeacon advised Peter that they had recorded their highest intake of donations from businessmen who had attended church for the right reason and that they would record the highest profit the church had ever made. The archdeacon informed Peter that he should be careful not to deviate too far from the Bible as criticism was being levied by an increasing number of the congregation as to the accuracy of the sermons being preached and that questions were being asked why this was allowed.

The archdeacon said, 'No doubt the ones who are complaining are the ones who give no donations or just put five dollars in the plate as compared to the thousands of dollars some businessmen have foolishly given us, thinking their good deeds will give them eternal life. These people want to sit in the church the rich have paid for and still want the same rights. They're joking, aren't they?'

Peter said, 'I must admit sometimes, I have lied, but only to the degree that what I have said is what they are already thinking. Yes, if I was a religious man, I most probably would follow the Bible like Simon, but I never have been. I joined the church to build this into an extensive business, not to serve God. One thing is for sure – the money that we have made would impress my father, the banker, if he ever knew about it.'

'I am amazed at the number of men and women who will allow you to rob them in the name of Jesus Christ and not think twice about it. The average person doesn't know anything about the Bible and most probably has never read it. All they want is for someone to tell them their sins are forgiven, and they are prepared to pay whatever price you ask. This is better than stealing as they willingly give you their money, and there is no comeback against you.'

'You know, if they really thought about it, they do not need us. They can pray directly to Jesus rather than through us. If they want to know what the Bible says on a topic, they can go to any number of books and read up on it themselves. But no, they rely on us, thinking we have a direct line to heaven.'

The archdeacon ordered another bottle of champagne, and they all took part in a last drink. They decided on a restaurant to go to celebrate their successes and paid the bill and walked to their car. All got in, and Peter drove out of the car park onto the freeway, with everyone being in a jovial mood and chatting about trivia.

Chapter 29

Monique, Simon's wife, was uptight. Bill was restless, and she had a bad day looking after him. She decided to take him around the block in a stroller (front-facing pram), hoping he would settle down and go to sleep. She put him in a stroller, took a bottle of water, and headed off.

Some teenagers drove up to the small self-serve store, parked their car, and went into the store.

They went up to the checkout and produced a gun, yelling, 'This is a hold-up!'

They grabbed the money out of the till. The manager saw what was happening and triggered the police alarm button. The robbers saw what had happened and fired a shot at the manager, missing him. They rushed outside and tried to get to their car. The police pulled up, and they fired at the police. The police returned fire.

Monique heard the sirens and the shooting and was crossing in front of the self-serve store. She ran, pushing the stroller as fast as she could without tipping it over along the uneven footpath. The robbers fired at the police, hitting one of them, and another bullet ricocheted off one of the police cars. Another bullet was fired, and it too ricocheted off the police car. More police arrived. The teenagers fired at the police, who returned fire. They shot one teenager dead. The other put his hands in the air and surrendered.

Monique kept running down past the self-serve store, pushing the stroller, and was puffing as she had lost her breath. Simon got off a bus and began walking home. He recognized Monique running towards him, picked up speed, met her – she was in a hysterical state – and grabbed her.

Monique, while sobbing, said, 'I was walking past the self-serve when I heard shots being fired. I ran to get Bill and myself out of the way. They were shooting at me, and I ran. A bullet flashed past me as I ran.'

Simon asked, 'Are you all right?'

Monique replied, 'Yes. Just shook up.'

Simon went to the front of the stroller to get Bill out and saw blood. He screamed out, 'they have shot Bill!' He grabbed Bill, but there was no life in his body. Simon realized Bill could be dead. 'God, no, please, no – not Bill!'

Bill's body stayed lifeless, and blood was still seeping out on Simon's hand.

Monique screamed, 'God, not my Bill! Please, Lord, not Bill!' and collapsed on the footpath.

The police ran up to Monique and saw what had happened. They called for an ambulance, which arrived within minutes, and immediately, the paramedics went to Bill and checked his heartbeat, but there wasn't one. They could do nothing. Bill was pronounced dead, caused by a ricocheting bullet from the gunman.

The paramedics picked up Monique, put her on a stretcher, sedated her, and took her and the baby to the hospital. We sedated Monique, as the medicos could not control her emotions and crying. Simon refused to leave her side and stayed with her in the hospital.

The whole instance made the headlines on TV and press and was the talking point on radio why God allowed an innocent child to be shot dead by a teenager. 'Where is God when you need him? If a minister is treated in this fashion, then the rest of us have no hope.' The radio blasted an inhumane God who would allow a disabled boy to die at the hands of two teenage murderers.

The next morning, Monique was brought out of her coma and allowed to confront what had happened to her Bill. Simon went to the hospital to bring Monique home and was confronted with her anger at how wrong they had been about God and how right Peter Sutherland was.

Monique said, 'What fools we have been about God. There isn't one, or if there is, what a blood-craving monster He must be to take from us the life of a disabled baby. A baby who didn't have the mentality to sin and yet paid the ultimate price for sin.'

Simon said, 'I don't have the answer. I have been asking the same questions, trying to understand why. But I cannot come up with a plausible reason. We are cursed or stupid not to see that Satan is more powerful than God. I don't know.'

Simon gathered Monique's belongings and her bag, and both made their way out of the hospital and to their car. They both sat in the car, and Simon started the engine and drove home, with nothing being said between them.

They arrived home, and Simon parked his car in the garage. Monique went into the house and was confronted by their eldest son, who hugged her, and both went on in and sat in the lounge. Simon came from the garage and sat down opposite them. Everyone sat in silence for about two minutes when, suddenly, there was a ring from the front doorbell.

Simon got up slowly and said, 'Who the hell could this be? Never mind. I will get rid of them.'

Simon opened the door to see Minister Bolton standing there with his hand stretched out.

Simon greeted, 'Hi, Robert. Unfortunately, you got us at the wrong moment. We have just arrived from the hospital and are not in any mood for chatter.'

Robert said, 'I can understand why, but thought you may be going through a process of turning against God and blaming Him for what has happened.'

'You are damn right there. We have had enough sermons on God and His love when in reality, He wouldn't give a continental about us or mankind.'

'Why don't you let me in and allow me to discuss the issues with you?'

'Not today, Robert. We really have had enough and are not in the mood to hear any more praises of God, not after what we have been through.'

'I can well agree, but I am sure that you have raised between yourselves many questions regarding the event and why the Lord allowed them to happen. At least allow me the opportunity to discuss them with you. I will be brief.'

Simon was just about to shut the door in Robert's face when Monique came to the door and said, 'Robert, we are not going to be pleasant to God or you, so we believe it would be best you leave. We really have had enough of religion and the "grace of God" philosophy.'

Robert said, 'I do insist you discuss your feelings with me. Otherwise, Satan, who is knocking at your door, will turn you against the truth and God.'

Monique turned and looked at Simon and then said, 'All right. Come on in, please, just for a minute.'

Robert came on in and sat down where showed. He then asked, 'What are you feeling at present?'

Monique replied, 'What are we feeling? You have got to be kidding. We believed in the Lord all our lives, and when we needed Him, He turned his back on us and kicked us in the guts.'

Robert requested, 'Can I have a drink of water?'

Monique went to the kitchen and brought him a glass of water.

Robert said, 'Thank you. First, who do you think you are in treating God as if He has taken one of your possessions? We were created by Him for His purpose and not yours. We are here for how long He intends, not how long you want Bill to be on this earth. You were expected to raise Bill and to ensure he had a Christian upbringing. At this point, most people fail, as they do not have a Christian upbringing themselves and therefore don't pass this on to their children.

'The second point you must consider is that God has not caused you grief. He knows what it feels like to lose a son. After mankind wiped Him to near death, he saw them crucify his own son. He is not testing you, but allowing you to see for yourself how much faith you really have in Him. Did you ever ask God to show you why he took Bill? Maybe it is something futuristic, and the reason is yet to be presented to you. But if you had faith, you would grieve for Bill's loss, but trust God as to the reason and rest assured that it is in your best interest. While it is hard, you remember Bill was under your stewardship but belonged to God. He was the one who gave Bill life, not you.'

Simon looked at Monique and said, 'No, we didn't think along those lines. We were overcome with grief, and our loss caused us to turn against God.'

Robert said, 'Start thinking about what life is going to be like without Bill. Monique was forced to stay home with Bill 24/7 and basically could go nowhere, as Bill took a lot of care.'

Monique said, 'He was my baby, and I was willing to give up everything for him.'

'Yes, to the extent of neglecting your other son. Where is he now?'

'In his bedroom.'

'Has anyone considered what he is going through this minute? No. All that you have considered is to turn on God and show you have no faith at all in Him. Your faith is on sand, not solid rock. You have turned against Christ with the shout "Crucify Him!" for what He hasn't done. Remember, the person who pulled the trigger is also one of God's creations whom He loves. It was he who pulled the trigger and not God. The person, like you, is one who also has free choice, and he followed Satan, not God, but God still loves him.'

'You're right. We better see if we can explain it to our son. Thanks, Robert, for coming over.'

Simon and Monique saw Robert out and went to their son's bedroom to discuss Bill's death. After an hour, they came out and went into the lounge.

Monique said, 'We better bring him along with us to the funeral parlour. Otherwise, he will think he is left out and doesn't have a say.'

Simon said, 'That's all right with me as long as he can control his emotions.'

Chapter 30

William, a truck driver for thirty years, was finishing his last delivery for the day. He was driving down the highway, listening to the radio. He thought to himself, *Who is the singer?*

Goodbye, my old friend
We will meet you again

William had tuned out as the traffic seemed to have sped up, and he was concentrating on the road. He came back to the tune on the radio. He remembered it was Carly Simon.

Life has been short
And we only have got to know each other
For such a short time

William drove down the highway, and it was getting towards dusk; the sun was setting. He thought, *what a beautiful sunset*, when a car dived in front of him and caused him to swerve. He could feel that he was losing control of the truck as it swerved down the highway side-swiping other cars as he tried to get control of the truck and get back into his lane. He realized he could not do so and tried to slow the truck down.

The truck hit the concrete divider in the middle of the highway and threw William out of the cab as it rose and dipped while it crossed a break between the centre barrier and in the path of the opposing traffic. The driverless truck missed one car, thundering down the opposing highway. It missed a second one and then hit a white BMW head-on and burst into flames.

William staggered to his feet and tried to walk forwards towards the BMW, but his hip could not take his weight. He saw the fireball, and it became more intensified, and in that split second, he thought he could see three people in the BMW, one woman and two men trying to open the doors. The fire forced a second explosion and then another and then a fourth, and the flames leaped up at least thirty feet high and fully engulfed the BMW. William could do nothing but wait for help.

The fire brigade arrived as the fire took hold. They hooked their hoses up, and the police arrived.

The captain yelled out, 'Can you get all those people out of here? The tanker is liable to explode and take them with it!'

The firefighters grabbed their hoses and concentrated on the water to the centre of the fireball.

The captain grabbed the two-way radio and said, 'Base, we have a tanker with petroleum on fire on the main highway, ready to explode. We need foam and backup.'

Within minutes, a large fire truck arrived with four backup units.

The captain ordered, 'Concentrate the foam on the centre of the blaze, and, the other trucks, concentrate on the peripheries.'

The men jumped into action, and they concentrated all hoses on the blazing fire. News trucks arrived and set up for a direct report.

This is Ray Brant, your reporter. 'We are at the scene of a horrific accident where a petrol tanker crossed onto the other side of the road and crashed into a BMW, killing all occupants. The driver of the truck was miraculously saved as he was thrown out of the cabin as the truck jumped the median strip, missing all other cars except the BMW.'

Sometime later, with the fire out, the captain and police moved in to see what had remained of the car and the people inside. They noted that there was nothing left of anyone in the car and that the car itself had melted into a heap. They found the number plate of the car some one hundred yards down the highway. It was ripped off during the explosions, turfed into the air as the tanker was ripped apart.

Ray Brant said, 'We have confirmed that the occupants of the BMW who were killed in the horrific accident were Peter Sutherland, a minister of the local church, his wife, and the archdeacon of the church. The fire was so intense that there was nothing left of their bodies nor the car that they were driving. All were incinerated in the car, beyond recognition.'

Chapter 31

The congregation sat down, and Simon moved to the pulpit.

Simon said, 'I have been approached by several of you, advising that you have heard some disturbing interpretations from other ministers regarding divorce, homosexuality, and idolatry. First, I believe that most of you have been reading the Bible for many years and know what it says about these topics. I sense that the purpose of approaching me is to play one minister off against another and, second, to see if I will compromise my beliefs. The answer is no. For those who are new to Christianity or require guidance, I will briefly cover the Bible's position on these topics.'

'The Bible's purpose is to establish the Word of God. Not to give a populous interpretation. Some ministers take a very lax attitude towards theology to get a larger congregation in order to contribute more money. Also, some ensure their congregation gets to hear what they pay for. At this church, the banker and money dealer here is God. We rely on Him and have faith in Him to guide us and our fortune. If we do not leave it to Him, He would overturn the tables. That's why we only have pews.'

There was laughter.

'We do not preach to be popular. That, of course, is clear in the fact that we have only a congregation of twelve.'

More laughter.

'As you can see, the reality is we have quite a few more than twelve. But we do have twelve saints, I have been told, and their generosity has not gone unnoticed.'

'Now, getting back to the serious matter of divorce. Divorces have reached an epidemic proportion, with two in every five marriages ending in divorce. This leads to a lot of anxiety and heartache, especially for the children. Parents rarely get off scot-free, and most times, we hear of one parent committing suicide, owing to the pressure or loneliness.'

'So divorces are not to be approached lightly. The Bible states a person can divorce when the other partner has committed adultery. It does also allow a divorce when the marriage cannot function, such as in instances of mental health, a genuine fear of one's personal safety in a marriage, and such uncontrollable instances. It does not allow a divorce at any other time. You basically have to make a go of it once you have maneuvered yourself into a marriage. To say that you can divorce because you have found another person who suits you better, or that love has gone out of your life or that you have drifted apart is not a reason to divorce, according to the Bible.'

'According to the Bible, except for those instances already mentioned, death is, in reality, the only way you can get out of a marriage, and that does not mean a planned or contrived one either. Marriage was meant to be forever or till the Lord calls one party to heaven. It is recognized that Moses allowed people to divorce when their situation did not comply with the Bible. The state allows this also these days. It still means that unless you follow the Bible, you will sin and will have to answer to God, even though you have satisfied the State requirements.'

'Our second point is idolatry. Simply put, if you have any god other than the God of the Bible, you are committing idolatry. So, if you do not have faith in Jesus but have faith in yourself, then you are committing idolatry. If gambling, sex, and pornography are what you live for and will go to any lengths to satisfy your craving, then that is your god. It is the thing or factor that governs your life, that drives you, that is the most important thing in your life.'

'Again, to make it clear, if you come to church every Sunday and, for one hour, say, "Yes, Lord" but, for the rest of the week, Jesus is not thought of or mentioned and if it's work, money, yourself, the promotion, or any other thing that takes the place of Jesus Christ, then you are committing idolatry. It is only when you say, "Lord, I have faith in you, even though things look bad for me," that you can say, "I believe in Jesus Christ and have total faith in Him." All other times, you're just testing the water, and God will have to do something to bring you closer to Him because you cannot do this yourself, and you are, in reality, in Lucifer's camp and not with God, or Lucifer is knocking at your door.'

'You are comfortable on the couch, with Jesus on call every Sunday, and you think all is well when, in reality, you have not achieved faith in Christ, only dipped your toe in the water which you may need later to suck on, to quench your thirst. So it is not complicated, and you don't have to introduce red herrings as what the rich man said to Jesus. In that instance, the rich man wanted to buy his way into eternal life, which a lot of ministers have offered to broker since the Renaissance Period. These days, we call them scams as all they do is make the person or their church very rich and turn people off when found out to be dishonest.'

'Job was also mentioned to me. It was said that God was harsh on Job. We do not know the full story here, as we only get snippets about what happened. It was Lucifer who killed Job's family, and yes, the Lord allowed him to do it. It is the same as someone stealing your young six-year-old daughter, and later, you find her raped and murdered. Who was at fault? The parent, God, or Lucifer? Invariably, the question is raised – "Why did God allow this to happen? Not that

I was so stupid in allowing my six-year-old to roam unsupervised." No, that is not considered. Nor is the question "Why did God allow me to have the child in the first place, only to take her away from me?" No consideration at these times is given that it is God's child and that your job was to bring her up. "No, it is my child, and why did God allow this to happen?"

'Getting back to God and the criticism against Him. Those who question God's right to do things or cause an event do not have faith in Him. They do not say, "I do not understand why this has happened, but I have faith in you to see me through this disaster, and I continually have trust in you, for I know there is a purpose in all things you do." No, they are not saying this. What they are saying is "Hang on – what the hell have you done without consulting me? I believe in you, and you treat me this way. Enough. If this is the way you want to treat me, then find yourself another person. I am out of here." Idolatry is any other god other than Jesus Christ. You believe in yourself but invariably blame God.

'In relation to homosexuality, the Bible is very specific regarding this. It makes it clear that it is not acceptable. However, throughout time, most ministers have adopted a position that all sinners are welcomed in church and will allow homosexual couples to take part in the service. Some will not allow them to take communion, while others will. Most will not agree to the marriage of homosexual couples. The exception to this is where a minister has not agreed to follow the Bible and performs marriage services, serving a different God from the one in the Bible. Unfortunately, they declare they are following the Bible, with several exceptions. In these regards, there are more exceptions than rules. This still amounts to those ministers deciding what is right and wrong and worshipping their God and not the God of the Bible.'

'We at this church will allow homosexual couples to take part in the service but will not agree to marriage or for them to be recognized as being married. Marriage, in our view, is the joining of husband and wife and not two of the same sex. To this church, that is a relationship recognized by law. There is little doubt the minority homosexual groups have made the most noise and the majority are split between Christian beliefs who have done little to address this issue and those who have no beliefs and an "I don't care" attitude as long as they are not approaching me.'

'The politicians are, unfortunately, more worried with the minority group as they know the Christians will do nothing and therefore not be a problem for them. They therefore put their energy and effort into appeasing the minority group, even if it means they are acting contrary to the teachings of the Bible. The politicians, through their action and allegiances, look more like Pharisees every day and less like Christians.'

'This now concludes the sermon.'

'Let us pray...'

Chapter 32

The new archdeacon had been elected and called a meeting of all the ministers in his archdeaconry.

He said, 'We are all aware of the tragedy that has befallen my predecessor and Peter Sutherland and his wife. I do not intend to labor on what and why this happened other than to recognize it as a tragic accident and not as some of you think – an act of God and retribution. I have heard the rumors that were being said at the time of their death, but I prefer to ignore them and allow the two men and Peter's wife to rest in peace at the judgement of the Lord.'

'Both men worked tirelessly and built this church up to what it is now, which is the largest, newest, and most supported church in the archdeaconries. No doubt it took a lot of ingenuity and effort to get those donations. The size of our congregation speaks for itself in that more people come to our church than any other in the dioceses, and we should continue to encourage them to do so.'

'I have been informed that on odd occasions, where it was to our benefit, you were told to deviate from the Bible's teachings and teach what was necessary to secure the funding. This will cease, and the Bible will be the centre of any future teaching and sermons. Not the modernity that has been taught in the past. We do not intend to give false assurances of eternal life when it is not ours to give, but seek guidance from the Bible.'

'I understand a minister was dismissed in the past for following the teachings of the Bible, and no one raised an objection regarding his dismissal. The minister concerned is Simon Fuller. I have asked him to consider re-joining our church as a full-time minister. This, no doubt, will cause some embarrassments, but I believe over time, we will be able to sort out any problems that may arise should he decide to join us as a minister.'

'There will be problems, no doubt, with the congregation in that they have, in the past, been given an alternative interpretation of the Bible, and now we will advise them of what the Bible instructs. I believe this is called a complete somersault. I am sure that we can overcome any problems that may arise, and I intend to leave it in your hands to resolve these should they crop up.'

'I would recommend that any minister who is not sure of what to say regarding matters of divorce, homosexuality, and marriage and other matters should reread their Bible to ensure we give patrons the right advice when asked. Any questions? Good. However, you all seem as if a bus has hit you. Never mind. I am sure you will get your heads around it or accept the truth and not a populist interpretation of it. I must leave. Thank you for coming.'

The archdeacon stood and made his way to the door and walked out of the meeting. Everyone sat quietly, staring at the walls.

After some time, one minister said, 'We cannot accept what the archdeacon has told us. We all lied to the congregation, as instructed by the previous management, and now we are left holding the bag. If we now tell people that your good deeds don't count, then they will ask for the return of their donations as we have misled them.'

Another minister spoke up. 'We will be considered as fraudsters, ministers who have not adhered to their faith. There is only one thing to do, continue the way we have and ensure Simon doesn't re-join our church.'

Another piped up and said, 'The alternative and honest thing to do would be to resign and leave the church.'

From the group came, 'That's not an alternative. What? Leave such a cushy job? You would have to be joking.'

There were discussions among themselves till finally, one of them said, 'Well, has anyone a better idea? No? Then we continue as previously and keep it among ourselves. If Simon tries to join us, we will make it clear he is not welcome here. Agreed? Then let's get on with it.'

They all stood and moved out of the room.

Chapter 33

Emily couldn't sleep. Her pains were getting worse. She threw the blankets off her and noticed the bed was saturated. She yelled out, 'Stephen! Stephen!'

Stephen muttered, 'What do you want? I have to get up early in the morning. Let me sleep.'

'Stephen, my water has broken. The baby is coming. Get an ambulance.'

'Get an ambulance? But this shouldn't happen for another week.'

'Listen, stop being so difficult and telephone for an ambulance.'

Stephen jumped out of bed and raced to the phone and dialed emergency services. He said, 'We are going to have a baby, and we need an ambulance.'

The operator asked, 'Who are we?'

'My wife.'

'Have the contractions started?'

'Yes, they're occurring every five minutes.'

'What is your address?'

Stephen gave her his address while trying to help Emily get her things together.

'We will have the ambulance there in ten minutes.'

'Good. Thank you.'

Stephen looked for their pre-packed bag and found it, and then realized he was still in pajamas. He raced to the bedroom, put on his pants and shirt, and slipped into some white runners. The ambulance arrived, and they took Emily to the hospital. Emily had twelve hours of labor and gave birth to a baby boy.

Stephen phoned his boss. 'There has been a spanner thrown into the works. I had to rush my wife to the hospital, and she gave birth to a baby boy. Yeah. Both are well. We are calling him Jo, Joseph, after his grandfather.'

Stephen worked throughout the week and went to see Emily after he finished work. On the weekend, he thought he would do the right thing and go to Emily's house and tell them about the birth of their grandson. He drove the three hours and arrived there late Saturday. He parked his car outside Emily's parents' house and rang the doorbell. Emily's mother came out and was surprised to see Stephen, didn't know what to say, and didn't want to say it was Stephen at the front door.

Emily's father yelled out, 'Who is it?'

Emily's mother replied, 'Nothing special! Just the neighbor! What's wrong? Why have you come here? You know the trouble it could cause.'

Stephen said, 'I just wanted to tell you, you have a grandson, and both mother and Joseph are doing well.'

'Joseph? Jo? Is that his name?'

'Yes.'

Suddenly, the door was flung open, and Emily's father was standing there. 'What are you doing around here? Just wait. I will get the shotgun and shoot you myself.'

Stephen said, 'You can save yourself the time. I only came here to tell you that Emily has had a baby boy.'

'What's his name?'

'Sunshine.'

'Sunshine? What a stupid name.'

Emily's mother said, 'He means Joseph.'

Emily's father said, 'Joseph? Jo? That's a good name.'

Stephen said, 'Yep. Well, I have told you, as I promised Emily. I will be on my way.'

Emily's mother said, 'I will come with you to help her get on her feet.'

Emily's father said, 'No, you won't. The boy's a bastard. His parents aren't married.'

Emily's mother said, 'They were married a year ago, so stop being an asshole.' She said to Stephen, 'Wait for me near the car. I won't be long.'

Stephen moved to the car, and Emily's mother went into the house. He could hear the screaming, and eventually, Emily's mother came out with a suitcase. She put it on the back seat, and they drove off. Three hours later, they arrived at the house, and Emily was surprised to see her mother there. She rushed out and gave her a big hug, and both walked into the house, with Stephen following with the suitcase.

Emily asked, 'How come Dad allowed you to come?'

Emily's mum replied, 'He didn't. I told him I was going and that's it. If he didn't like it, I wouldn't come back.'

Emily said, 'You can stay here for a while. Come have a look at Joseph.' She led the way to the nursery.

Chapter 34

Simon finished his shift and drove home. A letter had been delivered earlier that day to his home, marked 'Private and Confidential'. Simon looked at the letter momentarily and then opened it.

The letter read, 'We wish to advise that your lease of the hall will end in thirty days, and we will not be renewing it. We have noted the comments from other religious groups that they object to our committee allowing community assets being used to promote the Christian faith over other religions. We have noted these objections and have ruled that we should not use the hall for religious meetings. We would appreciate you removing all your fixtures and chattels from the hall by the end of the month.'

Simon showed the letter to Monique, who also found it hard to understand. It was Saturday, and Simon decided to drive to the hall to see the extent of what had to be moved. He was in the main hall, writing up his list of things that would need to go, when he heard a noise and saw that the committee president was standing in the doorway and then walked towards him.

Simon said, 'Mr. Weatherby. Simon Fuller. My church has a license to use these premises on Sundays.'

Weatherby said, 'Only to the end of the month. After that, you have to vacate the premises.'

'Why? Who has complained?'

'Well, no one as yet, but it was thought best to be proactive and to decide before we receive a complaint.'

'Are any members of the committee? Christians?'

'I doubt it. Most people aren't you know. Those who say they are Christians are being deceitful. They believe for one hour on Sunday, and thereafter, the faith goes out the window. You see it all the time. They are Christians but only have faith in themselves.'

'But you're a Christian. I remember seeing you at the services I held at St Andrews. Surely, in your position, you could persuade the committee to act in our best interest and support us.'

'I voted against renewing your lease. You see, I think all this religious stuff is, in reality, just rubbish. There is no God, or if there is, He doesn't care about us.'

Mr. Weatherby was getting aggressive and throwing his hands about while he was talking. Mrs. Weatherby came out of the kitchen and joined her husband near Simon. She took a seat next to him.

Mrs. Weatherby said, 'We had a beautiful daughter 23 years of age. Last year, we lost her, and my husband has never forgiven God for allowing her to be taken from us. It is not right that a child should die before their parents.'

Mr. Weatherby said, 'She was our princess. She would do everything for us and was always good to us and helped whenever it was needed. She was our pride and joy. She went with a group of friends to a concert and, after the concert, went to have a drink with her friends. She met a young man and, after everyone left to go home, agreed to go to his unit for a last drink and to look at his paintings. He was an artist. They offered her a drink which had some drug in it and which made her sleepy. When she lay down on the lounge, the young man tried to rape her. She was screaming, so he placed a pillow over her face to stop her. He raped her and then found out that he had also suffocated her. The matter went to court, and he got a six-year sentence for manslaughter. It has destroyed our lives along with our daughter's. We now have nothing. No reason to live. Therefore I voted against renewing your license. It is all a fraud on your fellow man. Just another business to get money.'

Simon said, 'I can understand why you have done what you have, but they have been for the wrong reasons.'

Mr. Weatherby blew his nose. 'Bullshit. You're going to tell me that Jesus cared for my daughter? If He cared, why did He allow that criminal to do the dirty act of raping her and then killing her when she objected?'

Simon said, 'First, you ask why God allowed this to happen. Well, we are all free to do what we like within the laws of the land. So if you decide to do good under His commandments, then that is your free choice. If you decide to follow Satan and do bad things, then you have made your choice. God will not interfere as the choice is yours.'

'You recall Cain and Abel. Cain slew Abel, and God did not interfere. Everyone must make their own decision within their lifetime. The only ones who receive guidance are those who have faith in the Lord and rely on His choice. Through faith, they can resist Satan urging them on and do God's will and not what Satan tells them to do.'

'The next question you asked was "Where was God?" He was right there at the scene, hoping that person would change his mind and not do Satan's work. He hoped the person would resist Satan, but what you tell me is he was not a Christian. I believe God would not have allowed your daughter to experience the pain of being raped and suffocated but would have taken her life from her body before that happened and carried it in His hands to heaven. Did your daughter have faith in Jesus Christ?'

Mrs. Weatherby answered, 'She believed in Jesus and had faith in Christ. She always said what Jesus has planned will happen and thanked God for that.'

'Good. Then she is in heaven, and when it is your time, you will see her again. Next, you asked, "Why?" These reasons are unknown to us, and as you know, we all must die eventually. However, I can only comment on what you have told me, and it appears that previously, you went to church, but in your heart, you were an idolater, not worshipping God but your daughter, as she was everything in your life. Your daughter was God's child, given to you to care for on behalf of the Lord. Not your possession. Without faith in Jesus and only Jesus, you will not have eternal life. It seems this may be a wake-up call to you.'

'I can only assume Jesus allowed this to happen as it was necessary and the only way to prevent you and your wife from going to hell for the rest of your life. Jesus loves both of you. He knew your daughter had faith in Him and would have eternal life. I assume He is trying to ensure you both end up in heaven and not hell.'

'I am sorry that you have bottled up so much hurt and have not found your peace in Jesus Christ. You have turned your back on Him when you should have sought answers from your minister. The trial you went through and are still going through is not for Jesus's benefit but yours. Jesus can look into your heart, and He knows whether you really have faith in Him. He doesn't need these trials to give Him the answer. However, you were a religious couple and thought you believed in Jesus Christ. These trials are for your benefit to allow you to judge for yourself whether you really have faith or are just play-acting or fooling yourself.

The degree and the length of the trial is what He deems necessary for you to make the judgement.'

Mr. Weatherby said, 'That is all very nice, but God doesn't know the pain He has put us through. We are still grieving and burst into tears when we think of our daughter and what she went through.'

Simon said, 'Mr. Weatherby, you must be kidding. I will have to get you a copy of the movie *The Passion*. It clearly shows what man had done to Jesus Christ before they crucified Him. He was innocent and told the truth and yet man whipped Him and put a crown of thorns on his head. God the Father, as in your case, stood and looked at what they were doing to His son. He would not believe the depravity of man had reached in his heart. The man had the right to decide what action he wanted to take. They disfigured His son before crucifying Him. They stuck a spear into His side to make sure He was dead. Yes, God looked on and saw what men are capable of. God will judge these men and the person who killed your daughter. This world currently judges them, but that is not where it ends. They will find eternal punishment in hell. I am sorry to hear of your daughter's death. It answers why you have taken the action you have. I urge you both to find peace with God. We will be out by the end of the month.'

Simon got up, walked out of the hall, and drove home. He looked at disused factories or halls for rent and found one. He noticed one was listed not that far from his place and drove past it to see if it would be suitable before haggling over the price.

Simon drove around the block and decided the building was a bit too big for their current needs. He noticed the front gate was unlocked, and the gate was open. He drove in and parked his car and walked over to the building, which had an open roller door. He peered in to see if anyone was there, but could see no one. He walked into the building and noticed it was very large and clean inside, and he thought, *this will be expensive.*

Simon waited around, hoping to see if there was someone who could talk to him, but, after a while, decided to go home. He was just about to walk to his car when he heard a voice.

'Can I help you?'

He turned around and saw it was John Phillips, the person who had helped him some years ago when he was broke.

John shook hands with Simon. 'It has been a long time. I haven't seen you for years.'

Simon said, 'Yes, John, it has been a long time. What are you doing here?'

'I own the building. What are you doing here? I understand they have evicted you from the community hall.'

'How did you know? I only received the letter this week.'

'Never mind. What are you going to do about it? There are a few halls that you may consider, but they will not let you hold a Christian service in them, as the rich and famous are doing their best to discredit Christianity. While Christianity is around, there is a conflict with the rich and famous who are trying to ensure mankind is not bridled with things like faith and commandments. Ethics can be manipulated to suit the times or the situation. Religion can't and becomes an obstacle to corrupt the population. The thought here is that if we can limit religion, we can eradicate it over time, or it will become so infinitesimal that it will not be heard, noticed, or recognized and will disappear.'

'I figured that out, and that's why I was looking at an unused industrial site that could be converted into a church or community centre. Hopefully to allow us to preach to an increasing congregation.'

'Like this one?'

'No, this would be too expensive for us, and it would take us a few years to fill it.'

'Forget about the expense. If offered to you, would you take it?'

'Yes, but how much?'

'I own it, so for the next few years, I am prepared to let you use it as a church with the same conditions that were previously stipulated in the hall. The scripture, according to the Bible, is to be preached and not like the garbage that is being preached at St Andrews. A cross is to be placed at the front door to tell everyone this is God's church.'

'Agreed. We will have to put in some offices and rooms so we can have Bible study sessions.'

'Leave that to me. I will do it in a fortnight. You can plan on moving in three weeks' time.'

'Thanks, John, again for your help.'

'Thank the Lord. I am doing this with His resources.'

'John, how come you always come to the rescue and know what is happening to us? You seem to be Mr. Fix-It, knowing exactly what we need. How come?'

'It will reveal all in time to you, Simon.'

Both men shook hands, and Simon got in his car and drove home to tell Monique.

Chapter 35

Simon said to the congregation, 'This is our last assembly we will have in this hall as we have been told our license to carry out our religious service will not be renewed. The authorities, it seems, do not believe they should allow the community to gather here for worship. We have, by the grace of God, found an alternate venue where we will meet each Sunday. It's not as prestigious as these premises are. However, with some paint and partitioning, we will make it work. One of our benefactors has been gracious enough to allow us to use a disused warehouse as a church without charge. There is ample parking there, and all are welcome. The address and contact details are up on the board, and I have uploaded these on the Internet. We will therefore assemble at the Warehouse Church of Christ next Sunday.'

'Several of you have mentioned to me you have tried to be a good christian and have found that when you do the right thing you seem to end up second best in life's contest, or if it is a deal, second best in the deal or always struggling to make ends meet. We never seem to get on top of things, or get in front, have a win, or quite make it and yet, others seem to achieve their desires seemingly with ease and without a problem and live in comfit and abundance. Why?'

'Well, no doubt you are looking to me for an answer after trying to come up with one of your own without success. There is no doubt you have some inclination why, but sometimes it is hard to put the pieces together.'

'Well, I will give you my thoughts, which no doubt will confuse you even more if you're not already confused. I hope that will not be the case.'

'As advised in our sermon some weeks ago, you are born into sin because of Adam and Eve's transgression, and we adopt the ways of this sinful world as we grow to adulthood. You basically do as the world does and adopt its principles, attitudes, thinking, dealings and ethics. Look around you, most people want wealth, assets, a simple life, a good job, no responsibilities, promotions and Lucifer also knows' that you want this. You must keep up with the Jones's otherwise you look like a pauper. So, to do this, you must do unto others as they would do unto you. Connive, cheat, steal, act unethically, live an adulterous life, see pornography and see molestation as trivial even though it ruins lives. Follow the teachings of the unknown rather than the Bible. Allow minority groups to rule. Adopt the ways of this world, as this is all there is.'

'God created this world, cleaned out sin from heaven and intentionally allowed it to establish itself on earth with Lucifer being nominated as prince of this world. The Bible and Jesus describe Lucifer as a murderer, a thief, a wrecker of lives, one with no scruples or honesty. This is the world Lucifer desired and has established and fostered on earth. You have been born into this and from birth adopt the world's principles and have aligned yourself with the way of the world and Lucifer.'

'In the past, God created the angels in heaven and found that one third of them were of sin. He decided that for his purpose he needed souls that would reject sin as they had experienced at firsthand what destructive force sin is and disunity that it brings to mankind.'

'Unlike the past, where angels experienced holiness and God's Grace and then could decide to reject this and turn to sin, we on this earth now are born into sin and must seek Holiness if we are to have eternal life. A reversal of the previous situation and a striving of something better if we so desire. God knows that holiness is of a greater benefit, importance and is enduring to mankind and therefore should be earned and not just gifted by Him to be disowned at a later stage of life. We are born in God's image and therefore seek his help and develop characteristics like him. He concentrated all sin on this earth and uses it to test mankind and allows mankind to see what destructive force sin is.'

'God also gave mankind a free will to choose whether he/she wanted to remain in the way of the world or wanted something better. To achieve this, mankind must do two things. First, reject the principles of this world in relation to sin as advised in the Bible and secondly to move to a relationship with God by calling upon him and adhering to his teachings.'

'There are only two gods governing this world. God the Father, the creator and Lucifer the prince of this world who lays claim to all the other gods like pornography, gambling, money, extreme wealth, you as a person, anything that takes the place of God the Father. Lucifer was the second highest-ranking Angel in heaven before they found him corrupt. All mankind bows before one or the other and declares him King. Lucifer knows that when you are born in sin, you adopt sinful ways and most likely will stay in sin, as this is the easiest option. You cannot avoid sinning in this world. It is second nature and everywhere. The only way mankind can get out of this situation is to seek God's help, strength and follow his teachings and have faith in him which Lucifer endeavors to prevent and tries to block you from doing.'

'Lucifer knows you better than you know yourself. Until you turn to Christ you are open for him to entice you, persuade you, cajole you, offer you what you desire as pornography, sex, molestation, assets, a good job, wealth investments, promotions, anything, and everything this world can offer. The reason being is to ensure you stay in the way of the world and do not consider the alternative.'

"If you have faith in Lucifer, he will come in immediately and ensure you get what you desire or something of equal importance to you, because if you get what you want you will have no need to consider God, as you will be satisfied. Lucifer does not give you the chance to consider the issues and then decide. He will try to persuade you, entice you and use any means at his disposal to ensure you achieve satisfaction and consider you have made the right decision and move. However, what you have gained may not be to your advantage or benefit and you may forego something more desirable or beneficial to you. Lucifer will fulfill your immediate desire and not worry about your long-term needs or your eternal life.

'You will come out looking best, as he will evaluate what you want to achieve and ensure you get it, even if he must arrange for the demise of your opponent. Yes, he will not stop at killing, as he did with Caine and Abel. Jesus described him as a murderer. He is there to get his man or women hook or by crook and nothing is going to stop him. If you're an old recruit, he may not worry about you until you show signs of moving back to Christ. If you are deep in sin, he doesn't have to worry about you drifting back and therefore you really don't need anything more to stay in his camp. He has you.'

'Referring to the Principle of Opposing Forces (POF), as you progress left, you will feel your soul objecting to the way of this world. Why? Well, you were created not by Lucifer but by God, and he still loves you and takes pride in you, even as you sin. He still believes you will come back to him and is prepared to allow you time to do so.'

'It is God that created you and has put you on this earth. Why? To give you the opportunity to learn one thing and that is to have faith in him which takes a lifetime to gain. During these years, he expects you to serve him as best you can. You were born in sin but must call upon him to help you move away from this position, as you cannot do it by yourself. It takes time to gain the faith in Jesus Christ, which is the paramount reason you are on this earth. Yes, the Bible states you're here to serve God, but you do this through your trials and the trials show you the degree of faith you have in Jesus. As they intensify through the years, your faith compounds and you're able to say, "Lord I do not understand why these things are happening to me or why you have done this to me, but I trust you to guide me to safety" rather than deny him.'

'Lucifer does not care about your faith. He doesn't need it. He operates on the dark side, the killings, thieving, raping, dishonesty, cheating side of things to get to you and give you what you want to ensure your part of his camp. He is not trying to train you, or have you aligned with him, none of that. He is there to get your soul, and he does this by giving you whatever the world offers and to ensure you continue to sin as the world does.'

'The question of faith goes to the core of the issue as continually you will look at your soul and decide whether you will accept the lies and unscrupulous dealings which you will be expected to undertake and take part in this world or whether you believe they are contrary to the teachings of the Bible and if they are what are you going to do about it? Are you going to continue with them declaring they are only minor or are you going to say I will abide by the wishes of the Lord and have faith in him to direct me?'

'If you have faith in God he will not rush in and fix things for you but step back, give you time and assist you to achieve what you want to achieve or direct you to an alternative decision which will be to your benefit now or in the future. It is through these instances that you learn to gain trust in God. You must ask God for help through pray otherwise God will step back and allow you time to decide. It is through your prayers that God makes his move to assist you. You must ask or the decision is left to you.'

'Why does God allow Lucifer's person to win or get the greater benefit? He doesn't. It is in the workings of the two spirits. God created man/woman in his image and therefore they have a free will to decide on these issues. God steps back and gives them the opportunity to decide and to call upon Him for help when required through praying. With Lucifer, he doesn't step back and allow man/woman to decide. He decides and goes for you if the opportunity arises. He will ensure you get the benefits, the prize, the wins, assets, whatever you desire as he is not concerned with your wellbeing and having the opportunity of deciding because he has done this for you to get you into his camp.'

'What is important to God and Lucifer? To Lucifer, it is you who is important to make sure you do not become a christian. To God you are important, for through the Cross he wants to give you eternal life and riches in heaven. Material things on this earth are not important to God as these will be given up at death and that could be as soon as a minute from now. To God, the accumulation of wealth can only be done in heaven, not on earth, whereas with Lucifer the accumulation can only be done on earth irrespective of whether they will end at death.'

'If you are a christian for one hour on Sunday and Lucifer's for the remaining period, then he will endeavor to do what it takes to bring you over to his side to ensure you don't move to Christ even to the point of ensuring you accept being an antichrist. In these circumstances, I can assure you of his help until you are permanently anchored in his camp and then you will see the consequence of his treachery, dishonesty and betrayal. Remember, it is never too late to turn to Christ if you are in this position. He will never turn you away.'

'Say you go for a promotion and the other person is a christian. Then Lucifer will do everything to ensure you get the job, even if he must arrange for the person to miss his bus to get to the interview or arrange for him to have an accident. The problem is that it may not be the best thing for you to get the job. You may have the job, but now find yourself working twice the hours to keep it and neglect your family, which could later end up in the family court and a divorce. You got what you wanted with lucifer's help but the consequence has led to your downfall. Lucifer has you, but you have nothing and have lost everything.'

'This is the unseen part of life and the most hurtful part for all concerned, not the victory at the beginning but the destruction at the end.'

'The question that must be answered is in whom do you have faith in. Either God the Father or Lucifer. If neither, then you basically default to Lucifer, for only those who have the Holy Spirit dwelling in them can have faith in God. The rest are still unsure what they want because they have not communicated with God or have a relationship with him. They basically are leaning towards Lucifer as their King and at this point can be said to be two or three left on POF scale. You either accept The Truth and declare it to be so or lies and falsehood and follow along this path that best meets your desire.'

'With God, this would not happen. If you believe in God, he will guide you to the best solution and if it is the wrong job, then he will let one of Lucifer's followers have it, if it meant you would lose your life, family, or your God. If it is the right job, he will make sure you get it if it is in his plan, bearing in mind he may have another plan for you which you haven't thought of or which has not been revealed to you. That is why you must have faith in Him and trust his judgement. Even if you can't see where you are heading. He will not lead you astray.'

'So, it depends which side of the POF you are on and how far along the scale you are, as to what type of treatment you get. If you are one or two left, Lucifer will try to satisfy your requirements to ensure you stay with him so you can move to entrench yourself into his camp by continually doing acts of sin to the point where you don't need God or even consider him, as the accumulation of wealth and assets in this world is more important to you then eternal life and rewards in heaven.'

'If you are right of the POF scale, God will guide you if He considers this is part of his plan and you must have faith in him to guide you. What you deem is in your best interest may in fact not be the case. God will guide you by the Holly Spirit to ensure what happens is in your best interest. It is by faith that you come closer to God, not by wealth, gifts or possessions, which are only the way of this world.'

'You, as an individual, are important to God. You are his creation. He does not want to lose you, but has faith in you to turn from sin once you have had enough of its destructive force. To Lucifer, you really don't count. All he wants is that you do not return to God the Father.'

'If you are part of Lucifer's team, you form in groups and associate with others of equal sinful nature to yourself. When trouble arises, you seek help from your friends or colleagues even if it means to lie, destroy evidence, intimidate witnesses, tell lies, adopt unscrupulous practices, to ensure you are not found out. Your friends who are also in sin are more than happy to lend a hand, as they consider it the normal practice of this world.'

'If you are a christian, you will find yourself isolated and on your own. Rarely does anyone offer to help other than show you to the door. Your friends will abandon you as they do not want to be associated with you.'

'When Jesus was at Gethsemane and the Pharisees and soldiers came with swords and torches, all his loyal followers fled. They ran away, and some that were held tore loose and left their garments behind to ensure they were not captured. No one wanted to be around Jesus. Not even his disciples.'

'Those that plotted against him put him on trial, but they did not count on the fact which was God had put them on trial. They assumed that because Jesus was their captive, tied and bound that they were in control. They were showing their intent and doing their deeds in the dark of night. They spat on Jesus and hit him, showing their superiority against a bound person. The people were in charge. They were the Pharisees. The religious leaders, people of authority.'

'You no doubt are wandering why am I telling you these things. What is the reason for giving you this background?'

'The purpose is to give you some indication of what will happen to you when you are confronted by persons who want to do you harm or take what you have or protect their own turf or you go against a non-christian or one with very little faith in Christ who wants what you have. This also comes to the point why do they do better than you a christian?'

'If men of influence or authority came after you, you find that your support base will move away from you for fear of the consequences and that you are left on your own to fight the battle. You cannot rely on friends, associates and should expect that they will move their support away from you and will distance themselves from you as his disciples ran from Jesus. Most of your colleagues or friends aren't like Christ, who will always be with you and there for you, and if you have faith in Christ, He will deliver you from the mouths of lions. They will desert you as there is no benefit for them to stay.'

'If you're a christian, then the first line of attack against you will not be based on evidence or truth but rather lies and humiliation. They will attempt to belittle you by humiliation to try to unstable your belief. You say you are a christian but....'

'When Jesus was brought before the Pharisees, it was done in the night on charges that were baseless, fabricated, false and based on lies. The truth was exaggerated and taken out of context, and circumstances changed to suit their purpose. They would not hear from other members of their rank protesting the lack of honesty and integrity, as this did not fit their purpose. It had to be done their way, as they already had in mind what they wanted to achieve. All they had to do was arrange for the mechanism to be put in place. What suited them they used and what was against their plan was discarded and never saw the light of day.'

'What Jesus said was irrelevant, and he knew it and kept quiet, as in your case, for what you say will be irrelevant. If you find yourself in this position, then you too will be treated in the same way. You will find yourself on a drummed-up charge or on one that will require you to show the charges brought against you are false, which in most cases you will not get the opportunity to prove. Remember mud sticks even if it can be washed off later, it still leaves a mark.'

'Those that ran away from Jesus or disassociated themselves from him to ensure their safety later came to their senses and asked for forgiveness for they knew better. In your case, this may happen after the dust has settled and not by way of help during the troubled period.'

'So, it comes down to what do you want in this life and after your death and who do you trust will deliver it, the Creator, or the Deceiver? If it is eternal life, then it is God who can only give you this. If it is trinkets and possessions that are of this world, to be lost at death, then Lucifer is the only one that will satisfy you. God will not give these to you.'

'If you believe you are in this world for a purpose and that is to do the Lord's work and be trained to have solid rock faith in Him, then God can only satisfy you and guide you on your journey.'

'So the choice is yours. What do you want from life? You cannot have both Truth and Lies. The Light or Darkness. Eternal life as opposed to Hell. You must have one or the other.'

'At the commencement, we stated that as Christians, we never seem to make good. It always seems a struggle. Why?'

'The obvious answer now that we have covered some of the material is who gets your souls. This world or the creator God. God is offering eternal life and a better future. Lucifer is offering a better existence on this earth, but no future. As his purpose is to satisfy you to where you will align yourself with him, he will ensure you get the goodies as and when you need them while you are here on earth before you die. God is not chasing after you to get you to believe in him. He is there if you want to have a relationship with him and he doesn't resort to offerings, negotiations, deals, promotions, sex or any other sin of this world. One is of the Light, the other of the Dark. One is demanding the other leaves it to you to make the decision which affects your eternal life.'

'God wants you to know about heaven and His promise of eternal life. Lucifer wants to discredit God by telling you there isn't one except him. He will tell you God died at the Cross but will not tell you that over five hundred people witnessed this and had confirmed and sighted the resurrection and this has been documented beyond doubt. Lucifer will tell you that life after death is a myth and there isn't any. God promises that those who believe in Him and have faith in Him will have eternal life and will reap their rewards in heaven. Lucifer will try to discredit the Bible where God says the Bible is His Word.'

'God is in the forefront of people's minds, even in the minds of atheists. When a non-christian gets angry, they move to blaspheme and use the Lord's name in vain, yelling "Jesus Christ" as if it is Jesus's was the cause and not them. You never hear a person blaspheming Lucifer or yelling out his name in anger or in vain. It always seems they used Jesus as the cause of things rather than Lucifer. This identity allows Lucifer to appear as if he is a mirage, non-existent, a connived spirit who can't be held accountable for the damage and destruction caused. In their minds, God is the creator and, therefore, the cause of all misery. It is therefore preferable to avoid God and do as the world requires to benefit and succeed and avoid being associated with the one that reaps havoc.'

'You must always remember that God had been treated harshly by the Romans during his crucifixion. They wiped him to near death, sat him in a corner bleeding and partly unconscious, placed a crown on his head and pushed the thorns into his forehead, causing much pain and loss of blood. They placed a purple robe on him and mocked him, spat on him and slapped him to show they were superior and in control. They weren't. What they were doing is laying the basis for their own judgement, for they would appear before Jesus after their death and no doubt would then plead for his mercy. When a non-christian or a christian start swearing in the name of Jesus or starts dumping vulgar language or blasphemes on Jesus, he is in fact joining the Romans in mocking Jesus and taking the superiority attitude which is Lucifer's attitude. A lightning bolt will not strike you at that point, which is a pity, as judgement would end there, but what you have said against Jesus will be brought up at judgement time and you will have to account for your actions. It may be brazened of you to use colourful language against Jesus in the presence of your mates, but remember, you uttered the words, and you will appear before Jesus to explain why and you will be alone cringing.'

'Life's benefits are reversed at death in that those who support Lucifer die with none of their assets and do not have eternal life, they lose everything all that they work for and strive to achieve in this world which amounts to nothing but those who have faith in Jesus find their richness in heaven and have eternal life to reap their rewards. The ultimate decision is yours to make with only Lucifer forcing you to decide, not God, who leaves the choice totally to you.'

'Lucifer cannot give you eternal life. In fact, he cannot give you life. He cannot resurrect a person. The only thing he can give you is what is here in this world. He offered it to Jesus when he was in the desert, which Jesus rejected. You too, should do the same. He can give you help to get what you want but will only do so if it is to his benefit, not yours, and can only offer things of this world. You get what you want to where you are immediately satisfied with him and will bow before him, declaring him King. A short-lived offering as Lucifer does not know how long you have on this earth. Only God does. What you gain by deceit and sinful practices may only be held for a day and then death befalls you and you lose life and have nothing.'

'The other difference as to why non-Christians make out better in this world is because they are not involved in trials. Only Christians have trials, for you must have the Holly Spirit within you before you begin your trials. Trials take up a lot of time in dealing with their complexities and agonies and non-Christians avoid these, leaving them time to enjoy their wealth, pornography, adulterous life, gambling and association with like mates. These activities take up the time that would be used or could be used in the past to walk with God. Since they have rejected Him, they look towards material things to fill the void as a replacement for God.'

'Christians, by their decisions, are walking with Christ and, therefore, are being trained in God's ways, bringing them closer to his image. God concentrates on the training, not the provisions of wealth, asset accumulation, sinful activities. His prime task is to train you to have eternal life, which, in itself, is a rollercoaster ride.'

'One thing that must be emphasized is that your walk with Christ will not be an easy one. The reason is there is no other way for you to earn faith in God other than through trust. God does not manufacture incidences. He controls nature and the elements of this world. For your training, he uses the events that happen in this world. He does not cause them or manipulate situations to make good. Lucifer will manipulate, connive, make you think different things, act differently, cause you harm, cause you to strike out to kill, but not God. He knows what Lucifer is going to do with you. He knows his plan and uses his conniving and scheming manipulation for your benefit. He does not run a tit for tat spiritual with Lucifer to see who can get on top. He knows what Lucifer is going to do and uses it for your benefit.'

'Trials are a walk with God. You learn to be guided by him, instructed by him, seeking his support and discuss your fears and challenges with him through prayer and trust Him. If you are only praying to God once a fortnight, then you are not in reality with God. You, unfortunately, are being conned into believing that God is there as and when you click your finger, which is a common deceit of Lucifers.'

'As you develop with God, there will come a time or several incidences which cut the feet from under you. These are heart reaching situations causing you to question the existence of God and the use of being a Christian. Be on the alert for these, as they will strike unexpectedly and will put you in a spin. You should recognize these for what they are. You have reached a point in your walk with God and believe that you trust God and have faith in him. God knows if you have but you think you have, but really there is nothing to prove it other than your heart.'

'Jesus had total faith in God the Father, yet at Gethsemane he prayed the cup may be taken from him. It wasn't, and they forced him to endure considerable humiliation, pain and torture both mentally and physically to prove to the father that he could and was willing to go through what they expected of him. He did not prove this to the father but to himself that he had total faith in God the Father and his outcry on the Cross "It is Finished" proved that.'

'Like Jesus, you will reach the point with God when you will be taken hostage by an event or an experience. Lucifer will manipulate and cause this event to prove to you-you are doing the wrong thing. Lucifer entered the minds of those who were attempting to arrest Jesus and caused them to think of crucifying him. He stirred the crowed up against Pilot, leaving no workable alternative.'

'You will feel isolated even if you are part of a family to the degree where you cannot find peace. As you are part of Christ and God the Father, you will be given the opportunity to experience some of the pain Jesus went through on the Cross. You, of course, will not be replicating the Crucifixion, for Jesus took all our sins to the Cross, including your own. All you will share is an insight into what Jesus went through in the lead up to and his subsequent death. Many have described they wish they died as the pain has been so extreme.'

'Most at this point will leave Jesus and run like the disciples did, declaring they do not know Him or, like Peter, who denied Him. You have heard it; what type of God would do this or allow this to happen? Few will stand their grounds and while they ponder the catastrophe at hand, the death of a loved one, the murder, rape, bashing of self or a loved one, bankruptcy, losing everything ever owned. Some like Jesus will look up to God and ask for his strength to get them through this ordeal as they have faith in him and know only he can get them through this situation.'

'Many will not return to Jesus as Lucifer has snaked them, "If there was a God, do you think he would have allowed this too happened to you" and like Adam and Eve, fall for his treachery. Others will, after a time, realise that they have failed themselves and return to Jesus to again try and find faith in him knowing what they have done and recognizing that they did not have the faith they thought they had.'

'The question asked at the beginning, while a simple one, needs consideration from several areas to answer, as to why non Christians seem to benefit and not struggle but christians do. It can be seen from what we have said that there are several reasons that cause this of which the paramount one is where you are positioned with God. Lucifer's purpose on this earth differs from that of Gods. God placed Lucifer on earth, not the other way around. Lucifer is here to be used by God to evaluate mankind, so they give the true believers an opportunity to seek God and walk with him in faith. This cannot be done without Lucifer for there must be an opposite too good for mankind to have a choice and an alternative so the thru believers can be found, nurtured and trained to have faith in Christ. Lucifer knows he is being used by God and has taken this time to ensure that all that are born in sin stay in sin and God does not get new recruits. The spirit that will give mankind the greatest material benefit on this earth is Lucifer. The one that will give you eternal life and rewards in Heaven is Jesus.'

'As stated, you will have to make one very important life and death choice, whether you believe in God and will have faith in Him or follow Lucifer. God will not make this choice or decide for you, but Lucifer will. God has given you the responsibility and authority to make this decision, as everything afterwards will be a consequence of your decision.'

'The real question to answer is, do you want to be part of those succeeding in this world while they are alive or those who have been promised eternal life and their rewards in heaven? Remember, success gained on this earth is never kept and you could exist but for a moment.'

Let's pray...

Chapter 36

Simon and Monique had arranged to meet up with Robert Burton to have a cup of coffee and to discuss what was happening around the traps. Simon and Monique waited outside the café "Anytime" for Robert and were enjoying the quiet and being out in the sun when suddenly, a woman ran past, chased by several men, yelling abuse and shaking their fists at her.

Simon moved out of the way, and the women grabbed one of the café's smaller tables and threw it at the man chasing her. The men stopped in their tracks, and she grabbed a rock from the curb and threw this at them while growling like a bear and seemingly foaming at the mouth and breathing deeply.

Simon and Monique had never seen this before and were frozen in their tracks, not knowing what to do or whether to get involved. Robert appeared while they were staring at the woman, who was moving back and forth uncontrollably.

Simon greeted, 'Hi, Robert. You have come at a bad time. There seems to be a commotion over the woman there being chased by those men, and they seem to be intent on doing her some harm. She seems to be mentally ill or suffering from some phobia, as her movements are very erratic.'

Robert said, 'No, she is not mentally ill. She is possessed, and no doubt has had a hard life being in such a state. Look at her eyes and her action. You can see she is under the control of an evil spirit.'

'What can we do? If they catch up with her, they will do her harm, as she doesn't seem to want to make a bolt for it. She seems to be hesitating, trying to move our way, but something seems to stop her.'

'Well, there is no way drawing a line in the sand will stop them.'

Monique stepped inside the café and signaled Simon and Robert to do the same. As they turned to go inside, the woman made a run straight towards Robert and grabbed hold of him and refused to let go of him. Robert put his hands on her head and told Simon to do the same, and both men prayed for the woman in Jesus's name. The woman was struggling, trying to stay with Robert while her body was trying to run away from him.

Robert said, 'In the name of Jesus Christ, I command you, evil spirit, to go out of her.'

Simon said, 'In the name of Jesus Christ, I command you – go out of her.'

They repeated the prayer for a minute or two, both holding their hands on her head while she moved erratically. Then suddenly, they felt something push past them with a force, and the woman dropped to the ground. The café owner, seeing what had happened, came out with a glass of water. They got the woman to a chair and helped her sip some water. They noticed she was composed and not acting as she had been previously.

They pulled up some chairs and talked to her. At that time, Monique came out and sat down with them. She seemed to become calmer when she saw Monique and began talking to them. She advised her name was Sharon, and that she had been in that state for about a year. At that point, a man came up to her and stood in front of her. Robert stood up, thinking that it was the man chasing her. He turned to say something to the man, but Sharon spontaneously stood up, and both hugged and kissed each other.

Sharon said, 'You must probably wonder who this fella is. He is my husband, Paul. We have been married for eight years and have two daughters, 4 and 6 years of age. About a year ago, something went wrong with me. I became aggressive, short-tempered, and would rave and rant and yell like a madman. I would become aggressive towards my family and parents and could not control myself to where Paul eventually had to take out an AVO against me to prevent me from seeing him and the children. Our marriage was being torn apart by the evil spirit within me. We both agreed it was the only way to protect those whom I loved. Otherwise, I would become violent towards them and hurt them if they came close to me.'

'Today I tried to get home to see my babies for the last time as I was going to kill myself to stop the pain and hurt and isolation. Paul saw me and yelled out to me. I picked up a rock and threw it at him but missed him and smashed the next-door neighbour's window. He came out, and I ran off with him after me, with his three teenage boys in pursuit. Paul took chase to make sure they didn't harm me. I stood my ground as the spirit in me did not want to be near you two men. I decided there must be something within you that other people did not have, so I tried to get to you, but the evil spirit in me stopped me from doing so until that last minute when I could run towards you, and you put your hand on me. The spirit fled as soon as you prayed, in Jesus's name.'

Simon said, 'Robert said that you were not mental, but possessed with an evil spirit. Where did you pick up this spirit that had entered your body? You don't seem the type who experiments or delves into black magic.'

'I don't know. I haven't done anything abnormal in my routine. Nor have I been overseas or any of the things you mentioned. I just don't know. I was a simple stay-at-home parent, taking the kids to school, doing the shopping, nothing out of the normal.'

Paul said, 'We are not a religious family and always were one of the first to criticize Christianity, declaring it to be a waste of time and that only fools take up religion. In reality, we did not want to be the odd one out, believing in Christ when everyone around us was doing the opposite. Now we give thanks to the Lord and can see that we were the fools being misled by the world. We are going to have to get back on course and follow Christ.'

Simon said, 'You see, that was one of your problems in that when you rejected Christ, you rejected the acceptance of his Holy Spirit. Without His spirit in you, you become an empty body for any evil spirit to take up residency. The evil spirit will never live where the Holy Spirit resides. He doesn't have to. There are plenty of other bodies out there with no protection, there for the taking – the non-believers, the ones with all the answers.'

While they were speaking, the police arrived and handcuffed Sharon. They knew of her violence, and she had been in trouble before with the police. This time, they were not taking any chances, as they knew how violent she could get.

One police officer said as they handcuffed Sharon, 'What is it with you women today?'

Sharon asked, 'What do you mean?'

'A complaint has been lodged against you, acting violently towards some men. You broke their window, and there has been another complaint being lodged shortly after we got here that a woman outside the courthouse smashed the windscreen of four police cars that were parked there.'

Robert said, 'Oh no. That means the evil spirit that went from you has taken up residency in another woman and is forcing her to do things she would normally not do.'

The police officer said, 'No, mate, just mentally ill. No evil spirits. You don't really believe in that rubbish, do you?'

The police grabbed hold of Sharon and escorted her to the police van and commenced to put her in the holding pen so they could take her back to the police station for processing.

Paul said, 'What are you doing? She is all right now. She is a different person from the one you know. She is not violent anymore. The evil spirit has left her.'

The police officer said, 'Sorry, sir. We have our orders. Just doing our duty. If you have anything to say, I suggest you say it to the judge tomorrow in court. It is his problem from now on. We only arrest people, not judge them. Just one word of advice. I wouldn't try the evil spirit argument. No one is going to believe you. In reality, we are all evil spirits these days, doing what we want to do with no thought of our fellow man or neighbours.'

They then took Sharon away in the police paddy wagon back to the station, where she was placed in a cell with other offenders who were to appear in court the next day.

Simon said, 'We will go to court tomorrow and explain things to the judge. Don't you agree, Robert?'

Robert said, 'You could end up being sent to a mental institution for examination. Do you think a judge would understand what has happened? Do you think he will take your word for it? No, we will have to pray for the Lord's guidance on this one?'

All three men shook hands and decided to meet at the courthouse the next morning and see what they could do to assist Sharon. All agreed that it would be an uphill battle to convince the judge of the truth and that they could only do this and not fabricate a story to get Sharon released.

Simon and Monique, still shocked, walked home, while Robert caught a bus. Paul walked home rather than catch a bus. All departed. None wanted to stay back for a coffee, not after this incidence.

Chapter 37

It was nine thirty in the morning, and Simon, Robert, and Paul were waiting outside the courtroom.

Paul said, 'Well, did anyone come up with any ideas that may persuade the judge? I went to the next-door neighbour's place and payed him for the damage Sharon did. He will not press charges today. That's one good thing.'

Robert said, 'Yes. I decided the problem is too big for us to handle and therefore asked the Lord to and handle the matter in His own way.'

Simon said, 'So did I. I couldn't come up with any answer or any argument that would persuade the judge. I too left it to the Lord to resolve in His own way.'

After about fifteen minutes, a court attendant opened the front doors of the court building, and people streamed in. Simon, Robert, and Paul went into the court building and looked up at the schedule on the wall and saw that Sharon's case was to be heard in courtroom 3 before Judge James Preston. They made their way to the courtroom, entered, and sat in the front row as it seemed everyone was filling up the back rows, most probably not wanting to be in sight of the judge.

At ten o'clock, the attendant yelled out, 'All rise!' and everyone got to their feet.

The judge entered the courtroom, stood at his bench, bowed, and sat down. He heard several assaults matters brought on by the prosecution and sentenced the accused to periods ranging from six months to a year in jail. The judge seemed not to be too sympathetic towards those being accused and was not in the mood to allow delays. He seemed to be intentionally trying to get through his caseload quickly, not worrying about the accused, just getting on with it as if it was a production line. They brought Sharon up from the cells below, where she was moved too early in the morning. They placed her in a glass case and told her to sit down. The door to the enclosure was locked by the attendant.

The prosecutor stood up and said, 'Your Honour, Mrs. Sharon Thomas appears before you on an assault charge and causing danger to community property. She has appeared before Your Honour frequently, and the last time, Your Honour advised her she would be sent to jail should she reappear again. She is now before the court, charged again with disturbing the peace and causing damage to property. We seek a jail sentence of between three to six months, Your Honour.'

Judge Preston asked, 'Who is representing Mrs. Thomas today?'

'I understand her lawyer phoned to advise he was ill and would not be appearing today. She is, therefore, unrepresented.'

'What about Legal Aid? Are they not able to represent her?'

'No, Your Honour. They are short-staffed and could not provide the resources to assist Mrs. Thomas.'

Judge Preston said to Sharon, 'Mrs. Thomas, please stand up. This seems to be a straightforward matter. How do you plead?'

Sharon replied, 'I don't know, Your Honour.'

'What do you mean, you don't know? Are you guilty of the charge or innocent of the charge? Did you do it, or are you denying the charges?'

'Everyone is telling me I did these things, but I don't remember ever doing them.'

'Are you saying you are insane? Is that what you are telling me? You do things but do not know what you are doing? Is that what you are telling me?'

Sharon appeared as if she was ready to cry. She mumbled out, 'I had an evil spirit in me' – she sobbed – 'that was forcing me to do those things against my will.' She then burst into tears.

Judge Preston said, 'Mrs. Thomas, I am going to send you to the psychiatric ward of the prison hospital for assessment and treatment and will reschedule a return date for six weeks' time when I have the psychiatrist's report.'

Robert stepped forwards. 'Your Honour, may I approach the bench? I believe I can help clarify what Sharon is trying to say. I am a minister of religion from the local church. My name is Robert Burton, and I have been a minister for over thirty years.'

Judge Preston said, 'I doubt you can do anything here, Mr. Burton. You are not a solicitor and therefore cannot appear nor advise the accused of her rights.'

'I am her minister and would represent her, as I believe she has no other. I was a witness to the events Sharon is accused of and can speak on her behalf and give evidence under oath.'

Judge Preston, in an agitated mood, not liking Robert's intervention as he wanted to get rid of Sharon's case and put it off to another day, pondered on what Robert had said and said, 'Well, all right. Can you please make it brief? I have several cases to go through today, and I am short of time.'

Robert said, 'Thank you, Your Honour. An unclean spirit possessed Mrs. Preston and—'

Judge Preston interrupted Robert. 'You mean Mrs. Thomas, don't you, Mr. Burton?'

Robert hesitated for a few seconds and said, 'Yes, I do, Your Honour. My apologies. An unclean spirit possessed Mrs. Thomas for about a year. If Your Honour looks at her record, you see that her continual appearance before the court started about a year ago. On this occasion, she ran towards me when I was having a coffee with a fellow minister and his wife. We together recognized she was possessed and placed our hands on her to force the unclean spirit to vacate her body. We placed our hands on her and prayed to the Lord Jesus Christ for His power to force the unclean spirit out of her body. And we did this through the power of the Lord. An exorcism, I believe, is the term, Your Honour. She is now not possessed and is back to herself. She has a husband, Paul, who is in court, and two children, aged 4 and 6. We ask that the court take this matter into account and release her from the charges laid against her.'

'Mr. Burton, I think you too should join Mrs. Thomas in being assessed by a psychiatrist. To tell me such rubbish is to say that I should pin your story up with the best that I have heard to escape prosecution. I am amazed that you didn't introduce a few angels to the story or some fairies. Can you come up with anything better than this, Mr. Burton? This is surely out of the pages of one of Disneyland's books or films, or are you trying to con the court? I am sorry, Mr. Burton, but I don't seem to have the imagination or tolerance for this garbage that you seem to have and what you have told this court.'

'It appears Your Honour is not a Christian nor believes in Jesus Christ our Lord.'

'No, I don't. Nor do I know anyone who does. But this is not something that prevents me from hearing this case. The doctrine of fairness forces me to give you the benefit of the doubt, Mr. Burton. I will adjourn this matter until eleven o'clock tomorrow, at which time you are to produce to this court the following witnesses for cross-examination – Jesus Christ, accompanied by any of His angels, if He wishes, and the evil spirit you have spoken about that was cohabitating Mrs. Thomas's body – as well as evidence that placing your hands on a person and praying shall force an evil spirit to vacate that person's body. Do you understand what I have asked of you, Mr. Burton?'

'Yes, Your Honour. I understand what you have asked for.'

'However, Mr. Burton, if you do not produce the evidence, I will have Mrs. Thomas assessed by a psychiatrist and have you held in contempt of this court. I adjourn this matter until tomorrow. Take the accused away. Next case.'

Robert, Paul, and Simon got up and walked out of the courtroom, and assembled outside the courthouse.

Robert asked, 'Well, I have really got us in a mess, haven't I?'

Simon said, 'No, you told the truth. No, we are not in a mess. Remember, Robert, when you came to my house when Bill was shot dead? That was the most frightful time of my life, and you told me to have faith. Well, this is another one of the Lord's plans, and I, for one, will not give up my faith in Him. He has a plan, but we just don't know about it. Despite that, I will pray for His mercy and help and rely on Him to resolve this problem that seems unresolvable by us. Let us pray to the Lord.'

They each stretched out their hands and overlaid one on top of another.

Robert prayed, 'Father, we are in desperate trouble in that they have asked us to have you appear in court before the judge Preston tomorrow. We are out of our depth in this matter and seek your guidance, intervention, and divine help. Amen.'

All men shook hands and went off on their separate ways.

Simon arrived home after about an hour of traveling and was immediately greeted at the door by Monique, who wanted to know what had happened. She could see from his expression that things hadn't gone well. Simon went into the lounge room and sat and stared out the window for a few seconds and then told Monique what had happened and the judge's demand that Jesus appear as a witness tomorrow for cross-examination.

Monique asked, 'What are we going to do? She is innocent of the crime. To say Jesus is to appear before the judge is an insult. What are you going to do?'

Simon said, 'What can I do other than pray and have faith in the Lord? We can only leave the matter in His hands and have faith that He will resolve the problem His way and in His good time. There is nothing any of us can do to satisfy the judge's demands. He won't accept our word what had happened and had even accused Robert of making up the story to persuade the court of Sharon's innocence. We cannot explain to him or convince him of the power of the Lord. He is not a Christian and, by his words, has mocked the Lord. I can only pray and leave the matter in God's hands.'

Chapter 38

Robert was sitting inside the courtroom, waiting until Sharon's matter was called. He had noticed the aggressive attitude adopted by Judge Preston towards those being accused or sentenced before him. He thought that Sharon should have been sentenced yesterday as she would get double today.

He was joined by Simon and Monique, and a bit later by Paul. There wasn't enough room for everyone to sit inside the courtroom, so Robert signalled for everyone to go out into the hallway, and they all moved out under the watchful eye of Judge Preston.

Robert said, 'Well, Simon, Monique? Anything?'

Monique said, 'We have prayed a lot and believe in the Lord and have asked Him to handle the matter. We have faith in Him.'

Paul said, 'I'm new at this, so I don't know what to do other than pray a lot and ask for the Lord's help as best as I can.'

Robert said, 'So have we all? Amen. I believe Sharon is next. We better go in and face the music.'

They all went into the courtroom, which was packed, and there was nowhere to sit, so they stood in the aisle. Sharon was told to sit in a glass box after being brought up from the cells below. They locked her door from the outside. She appeared nervous and had an awful night in the cells and was still crying when they brought her up. She looked at Paul and threw him a small kiss.

Judge Preston asked, 'Well, Mr. Burton, would you like to approach the bench?'

Robert moved towards the bar table and stood.

Judge Preston asked, 'Have you got the evidence that I requested, Mr. Burton, or are we going to have a swarm of locusts appearing in the courtroom? If you have, please have the evil spirit go into the witness box.'

Robert said, 'Your Honour.' He then paused for a minute, praying under his breath.

Suddenly, the courtroom doors were flung open, sending Simon and Monique flying to the front of the bar table, where Robert was standing. The doors were ripped off their top hinges and secured only by the bottom hinges. Other people in the courtroom were knocked to the ground or over people who were seated.

A young woman with a baby that appeared to be only a few weeks old tried to get up to get out of the way. At the entrance stood a woman with her arms stretched out, who grabbed the baby from the mother of the child and held it up above her head. She yelled out something, but it was more of a groan, not a word. She ground her teeth and again let out groans and spat at the mother she was trying to take the baby from. She pushed the mother away with extreme force, throwing the mother to the ground.

Police flooded into the hallway and into the courtroom with guns drawn. The woman threw legal reference books that were on the bar table at them and anything she could get her hands on.

Judge Preston asked, 'Cheryl, what are you doing? Where have you been for the last two days? Look at you. Put the baby down and go home and have a shower.'

Cheryl held the baby in one hand and was ready to throw the baby at Judge Preston.

The police prepared to fire, but the judge yelled out, 'Don't shoot! That's my wife!'

Robert looked at Cheryl and realized she had been possessed by an evil spirit, possibly the same one Sharon had. He approached Cheryl, who was preparing herself to take a swipe at Robert.

Robert said, 'In the name of Jesus Christ, I command you to put the baby down.'

Cheryl hesitated, and Robert grabbed her just as Cheryl dropped the baby. Monique dived and stopped the baby from hitting the floor, but hurt her knee. Momentarily, she held the baby in one hand while supporting herself with the other. The mother ran up and took the baby from Monique and ran out of the courtroom.

Simon grabbed hold of Cheryl, and both he and Robert prayed out loud to the Lord to expel the evil spirit. Judge Preston looked on in amazement, not believing what he saw. After about thirty seconds of praying, there was a loud smashing noise, and the evil spirit fled from Cheryl and went straight through a wall of the courtroom, leaving a big hole in the wall, while Cheryl collapsed onto the floor.

Judge Preston raced up to his wife and yelled out, 'Call an ambulance!'

The police put their revolvers back into their holsters and tried to pick up the chairs, books, and records Cheryl had thrown around, which were still on the floor. Robert and Simon tried to get her up and sit her down on a chair when the paramedics arrived. They gave Cheryl some smelling salts, and she came around.

Cheryl asked, 'Where am I? What's happened?'

Judge Preston said, 'Don't you know you did all this?'

'Did what? I didn't do anything. I was walking to the courthouse to meet you two days ago, and that's all I remember.'

Robert asked, 'Are you a religious person, Cheryl?'

Cheryl said, 'No. James would allow none of us to have anything to do with religion. In fact, our eldest son had to run away from home some five years ago to become a minister in another state because of James, and he refused to go to his wedding because it was to be held in a church and he believed in God. None of us could see any of the grandchildren. We had to stop communicating with him because of James.'

'Cheryl, the evil spirit could enter you and set up home because there was no Holy Spirit in you to prevent this from happening. I suggest no matter what your husband says, take a trip to see your son and explain what had happened to you, irrespective of whether James comes with you.'

After about an hour, the court was resumed, and Judge Preston ordered Sharon back into her glass box. Robert was at the bar table, and Simon, Paul, and Monique were seated in the courtroom. Unfortunately, they could not repair the doors, which were just about torn off their hinges.

Judge Preston said, 'Mr. Burton, I demanded that you produce three items of evidence to this court so we may judge the validity of the arguments you presented to us. I am satisfied that each item of evidence has been produced, and therefore, I am satisfied that Sharon Thomas is not guilty of the charges laid against her and of all other charges that have been laid against her this year. I therefore cancel all charges made against her, including the AVO, and order her immediate release.' Judge Preston then stepped down from the bench and approached Robert, who was just about to get up and leave with Simon and Monique. 'Mr. Burton, I need your service. I have messed my life up completely, thinking religion was all rubbish – nothing to it, just smoke and mirrors

– but today has shown me otherwise. I need your help to find God and to help unite my family if they want to know me.'

Robert said, 'Tomorrow is Saturday. I will come by about two in the afternoon if that is all right, and we can discuss the matter.'

Sharon said, 'Thank you both for all you have done. I already gave a prayer of thanks to the Lord for overcoming what seemed the impossible. They are preparing my papers, so I will have to stay here with Paul for about an hour. Can we come to your church on Sunday?'

Simon said, 'Of course you can, but in the meantime, don't forget to put a plaque on the front door reading 'God's Home' or something like it with a cross on it. It will show you are a Christian and help spread the word.'

Judge Preston said, 'That's a good idea. I will get one for my house.'

About an hour later, Sharon was released from the cells and was free to go home. Paul had got the car and was waiting when Sharon came out of the courthouse and sat in the passenger's seat of the car.

Paul asked, 'Is everything all right?'

Sharon replied, 'Yes, the papers are all completed, and I am a free jailbird. That's not my problem. How are the kids going to take me after I scared them so much? Maybe I should go to a hotel and see them later on, an hour at a time over several days or weeks. They may have nightmares if I am in the house at night, thinking, "She might come and hurt us during the night.'

'No, we will not beat about the bush. We are going to tackle this head-on. We are going home, and we both will face the music.'

'Don't you want time to remove your mistress before I move in?'

'No, both of you can sleep in my bed.'

They drove for about an hour, and Sharon knew they were getting close to home. Paul stopped the car in the driveway and got out. They were home. Sharon sat in the car, not knowing what to do or say, confused, not sure how she would cope with the kids.

Suddenly, there were screams from the house.

'Mum's home!'

They flung the door upon, and two girls raced towards the car. Sharon spontaneously got out of the car, and the girls hugged her. She knelt down and kissed them and burst into tears. She lifted them up and carried them into the house, with Paul closing the front door behind her.

Chapter 39

S unday morning service at ten at the new church. Simon steps up to the pulpit.

Simon said, 'Well I see everyone found where to go and I hope you have had the chance of exploring and have found where the teaching rooms are and facilities. You can see we have more of an opportunity to conduct bible studies here and have meetings and group meetings, so I think long term we will settle in nicely.'

'Before proceeding, I would say that we should give a special thanks to our benefactor John Phillips, who has kindly made this factory available for our use and has fabricated the library and meeting rooms and painted everything for free. I would ask that you include him in your' prays and thank the Lord for sending him to us in our hour of need.'

'I was uncertain what I should say at our first meeting here and finally decided that it would be appropriate to summarize how I see the world as it is today and the conflicts facing the church. It may seem a bit of a stretch to use Sodom and Gomorrah as an example and a warning to us, yet that is exactly what Jude did in the Bible, and we must take heed of this warning. One of the most obvious reasons that we are to remember in this biblical account of sin and judgement is that it is prophetic of the condition of the last days. Jesus said, "In the last days, it would be as it was in the days of Lot." Therefore, we must go back and look at Lot's time and see what the prevailing sins of that culture were. God is warning us that in the last days, there is going to be greater immorality.'

'I cannot think of a time when I have seen greater immorality amongst those who claim to be followers of Jesus Christ. I cannot think of a time when I have seen more open and blatant sin taking place by those who profess to be followers of Jesus. People who have walked with the Lord for years and those who have been ordained as ministers, who should know better.'

Dissolving marriages with no biblical grounds whatsoever. Willfully and deliberately breaking His commandments. Ministers of religion accused of molesting children in their care. Doing the very thing that Jude is warning us about. What is happening in the world and what mankind is doing to the planet shows us the complete relevancy of his words to us today. We immediately think of immorality when we speak of Sodom and Gomorrah. Certainly, that was a characteristic sin of these wicked twin cities. There were other things at the root that led to these sins that I would like to identify because it applies to us and our nation today. We know that the sin of Sodom was so great that the Bible says it cried out to God.

'Remember, when Cain slew his brother, God said, "What have you done? Your brother's blood cries to me from the ground." Think of all the sin that must be crying out to God right now in our country alone. The cry of the aborted child. The cry of those who have been murdered or victimized. The cry of the wicked and perverse acts that have been perpetuated upon our children and, most times, by those of the church and others in authority. The cry of the starving while billionaires flounder their money on trinkets to satisfy themselves without a concern for the welfare of their fellow man. These and other sins cry out to God. They are heard every single minute every day.'

'Look at Sodom and Gomorrah and then look at us in our country and all that we have been exposed to and the course that so many are taking and their attitude towards God. We probably would think, "Did the inhabitants of Sodom and Gomorrah really know any better? After all, weren't they basically pagan people with no knowledge of God?" No, they were not. It might surprise you to know that Sodom and Gomorrah had many religious persons who represented God to them, as we have today. As we go back to our studies in Genesis, we remember that the four kings of the East under Chedorlaomer defeated them, and it was God, through His servant Abraham, who rescued them and delivered them from their slavery. They had Abraham there to witness, to them, the true faith in God.

'When we think of Sodom, we think of sexual sin. But let's consider some things that led to it, and I think we might find a parallel in our own country. Isaiah 1:9–10 and Isaiah 3:9 tell us that there were all kinds of wickedness in Sodom. Jeremiah anchors it down to these two sins. Jeremiah tells us that the two primary sins of Sodom were adultery and lying. Can you see any parallel with our own nation today? What have we been hearing so much about for the last year and a half thanks to our politicians and some broadcasters? Adultery and lying. We have heard the rationale that it is OK to lie about this because we are told that everybody lies about sex. No one tells the truth. It is understandable. No one is going to tell the truth, even if you are the highest elected official in the country, even if you are perjuring yourself. It is OK to lie about sex. Somehow, we are going to turn a blind eye to that. Adultery and lying. These things are so commonplace in our culture today.'

'Listen to God's assessment of their sin in Jeremiah 23:14 – "Amongst the prophets of Jerusalem, I have seen something horrible. They commit adultery and walk in lies. They also strengthen the hands of evildoers so that no one turns back from his wickedness. All of them are like Sodom to me. The people of Jerusalem are like Gomorrah." God was reproving His own people. He is saying, "You are acting like the people who lived in Sodom. What is wrong with you? You are immoral, and you are lying about it."

'Then we have a different view on the sins of Sodom over in Ezekiel 16:49. He says, "Look, this was the iniquity of Sodom. She had pride, fullness of food, and an abundance of idleness. Neither did she strengthen the hand of the poor and needy." God says that she had pride, fullness of food, and an abundance of idleness. She was proud. She had more food than she needed. She never helped the needy. There was too much time on her hands. What an accurate example of our own country today. Interesting – the pride of those who lived in Sodom would be a nationalistic pride. Sodom was a city state. Their own kingdom. They felt strong and indestructible. Many feel that way about their own country today. We have been declared the only true superpower left on the face of the earth because of our incredible technology, economy, and so forth. We feel confident that no one could ever bring harm to us. We are feeling pretty good about ourselves in a world where things are not going as well, like in Europe.'

'The problem is that we have forgotten God. The Supreme Court recently ruled that it is against the law for a student to get up and pray before a sports event. We cannot teach scripture in our schools but must teach ethics. What a travesty of justice. What a slap in the face of our forefathers and all in the separation's name of church and state, which was merely something that was established that would protect the church from being interfered with by the state. That is the very thing that is happening right now. The state is now regulating what can and cannot be done by religious bodies or churches. The idea was not to keep the church out of the state, but unfortunately, this appears to be the case these days.'

'As you look at the documents of our founding fathers, you see the name of God invoked constantly, the Bible referred to also, even Jesus Christ, our Savior, mentioned specifically. Clearly, the church influenced the state. The idea of that separation was to keep the state out of the affairs of the church and not to keep the church out of the affairs of the state. Yet we have twisted it, and now it has come down to that you can't even pray at a sporting event or teach scripture at schools. It is an amazing thing, how we continue to thumb our noses at God and believe we can continue to do so without retribution.'

'In the 1830s, a historian named Alexis de Tocqueville came from France because he wanted to know the secret of America's greatness. He wrote a book called *Democracy in America* in 1831. He wrote these words that now have a prophetic ring to them. "Not until I went to the churches of America and heard her pulpits aflame with righteousness did, I understand the secret of her genius and power. America is great because of this. If America ceases to be strong in faith, she will cease to be great." I fear the day that he was speaking of has come upon us. You see, the sin of homosexuality and other types of perversion of God's natural order accepted by the state and forced upon the population are the beginning of the complete moral and spiritual bankruptcy of our nation.'

'That is what is happening in our culture as we have done our level best to push God out of our school system, out of the courtroom, out of the culture, out of our lives. We are seeing it shown in our society today with the breakdown of families and Christian beliefs. We are shocked when kids pick up guns and blow one another away on campuses. We were shocked recently to hear about the manslaughter in New Zealand by a single gunman. We are surprised when people live in immorality. It shouldn't surprise us at all.'

'It is all given to us there in Romans 1, where it shows the regression that sin can lead an individual or a nation to. Romans 1:21 says, "They knew God, but they wouldn't worship Him as God or even give Him recognition but thought of foolish ideas of what God was like." This is just what we have done today. Evolution comes to mind. "The result was their minds became dark and confused. Professing to be wise, they became fools. So, God let them do whatever shameful things their hearts desired. As a result, they did vile and degrading things with one another's bodies. Instead of believing what they knew was the truth of God, they deliberately believed lies. They worshipped the things that God made but not the creator Himself."

'Therefore, God abandoned them to their shameful desires. Even the women turned against the natural way to have sex and instead indulged with sex with one another. The men, instead of having normal sexual relationships with women, burned with lust for one another. Men did shameful things with other men and, as a result, suffered from diseases such as AIDS. When they refused to acknowledge God, He abandoned them to their evil minds and let them do things that should never be done. There are people today who will tell you this is not what the Bible teaches. The Bible teaches we should be loving and compassionate. "Some people are born gay. There is a gay gene. There is nothing you can do about it. That is just how it is." Not according to the Bible. There is no such thing as a gay gene, and the propaganda is thrown at you to give you an excuse to abandon your faith if you had it. If you never possessed it, then this will be a substitute for it. Lucifer's gift to you.

'We are born with a God-given sexual drive. When we lust after a member of our own sex, it is a twisting of God's natural order. But don't say this is what the Bible teaches, and this is compatible with Christianity. It is not. It contradicts what the Bible clearly teaches. We should have compassion for any person. I am compassionate towards a person trapped in a homosexual lifestyle. I am compassionate towards a person who is caught in any kind of sin. I don't think that we as the church should hammer people who are in this lifestyle. At the same time, we need to see what it really is, identify it for what it is, and thankfully tell people that there is deliverance through the power of Jesus Christ. I know many people who have turned from this lifestyle and have been gloriously delivered and transformed by the power of God. This results from the breakdown that starts with the wrong ideas about God and progresses to "self" and only self, doing as you please without limitation. Not according to the teachings of the Bible.'

'This brings us back to the importance of theology and doctrine. If we don't know what the Bible teaches or don't care, we get this warped, wimpy concept about God where, in the name of love and compassion and sensitivity, we set aside what the Bible clearly teaches. I am all for love. Don't get me wrong. But love properly interpreted. As I have said before, the rivers of love must flow within the banks of truth. There can be some crazy things that we can do in the name of love. We must have truth, have our doctrine in order, and then understand how that love is to be shown. Again, the illustration of Sodom and Gomorrah. They knew better, but they rebelled against God, and judgement came upon them.'

'Where does this lead us? What we are saying is that in place of all these sins and crutches we lean on and use as excuses, we should abandon them and kneel before God and give thanks and ask for forgiveness. We should trust in the Lord and have faith, even when it seems that things will never get better and will only get worse. You cannot change a thing, yet He who created the world can. Allow the train to hurtle towards you while you are strapped to the line of misery. It will not run over you, for the Lord protects you. All that it will do is force you to change your underpants, not your God or your faith. Do not follow the way of this world and think you can have one foot in each camp. You can't. You either believe in Jesus Christ as our Lord and Savior or Lucifer. There is no in-between. This is the ultimate choice mankind must make as individuals. The decision will govern your life after death.'

'The last point I want to raise is that of defending Christianity. We often hear criticism levied against the church and God. Rarely do you see anyone stand up and defend the faith. Yes, you see the pope and the heads of the Anglican Church and Muslim mosques standing up and uttering a few words in defense of religion while wearing their official robes, but rarely do you see them taking the issue up to the perpetrator. You don't see them on daytime television debating the issues, raising their objections, and holding the perpetrators of the misinformation to task or even naming them. It is clear they are glad to get away from the cameras and publicity, rather than defending the faith. We have, in this country and throughout the world, many academics in universities, colleges, and seminaries with PhDs, but rarely do we hear them step up and debate the issues in defense of religion or Christianity. They are paid as professors or teachers of theology, yet you don't hear from them. On the surface, most are not real Christians. Nor do they have faith in Jesus Christ, for they are the ones with the knowledge yet refuse to rock the boat for fear of their job.'

'Show your belief when the opportunity arises. "Step up for Christ when it is needed" is what you hear from the church, and they directed this to the parishioners, the ones with the belief but not the skill or knowledge to defend the faith. Those who have these skills are unfortunately not willing to risk their employment in defense of the faith, yet are quite happy to earn an income from religion and allow the erosion to continue. Revelations tell us that this problem will not go away but will become a tsunami as time goes on, with the Christian being very much the minority and persecuted.

'There is little doubt that the Christian faith will encounter choppy waters as we move through time and will need Christ to quieten these stormy waters. Revelations predicted that in the last days, there will not be too many left of the faith. When this happens, is in mankind's hands, for if we do nothing, it will be soon. However, if we stand up for the faith and say, "Enough is enough, and I, for one, will not allow further erosion of the faith," then we have stopped Lucifer in his tracks and endeavored to allow the new generation the opportunity God gave us. We continually hear from the men of science telling us about climate change and its dire consequences if we do nothing, yet we do not hear a peep, let alone a greater voice, from men of religion declaring what will be the consequence to our way of living, to our communities, to our country should we do away with God and try to substitute His Word, His teachings, with imitations and State laws.'

'Let us pray . . .'

Chapter 40

There was silence except for the sound of a helicopter propeller. 'This is Ray Brant in our news helicopter, hovering over the scene after the tornado rolled through the district, cutting a path of destruction. The tornado came from nowhere and was not even picked up on the news until it was too late and upon us. As I look down, we can see the destruction of all homes and power lines. Street after street has been hit with a massive force, with nothing left standing. The churches that were landmarks in our neighborhood have been flattened and destroyed.'

'The prestigious church St Nicholas, which recently underwent a multimillion-dollar renovation, has been flattened, as has been St Andrews Church. These were structures that were meant to last. On estimate, we believe approximately two thousand homes have been destroyed, and all churches and halls have been wiped from the face of the earth, including the council chambers and halls, with not one standing.'

'We are now hovering over my house and you can see like all the others it has been flattened completely with not even a tree standing.'

'We are now where the town centre used to be and are moving to the east, where we notice that there is a factory building still standing, as if the tornado has totally bypassed it. We notice that in this part of town, there are several houses still standing and again, as if nothing has touched them. It seems the tornado has avoided them. They don't seem to have any debris scattered around their yards, yet their neighbor's houses are flattened with debris all around. It is amazing that out of some two thousand homes that have been destroyed, thirty and an industrial warehouse still stand untouched.'

'We will hover over one of these homes and get a closer look to see if the tornado has affected them. The first one seems untouched. So does the second one. It seems that none of them have been touched at all. We can't see why they have been spared while all the other homes around them have been flattened. Not even the crosses on their doors or their plaques about God have been damaged or even pushed out of alignment or thrown off their walls.'

'We are hovering above the industrial building, the warehouse, and notice it too has a cross on the front door. Strange. We cannot come up with any reason these thirty houses and one industrial warehouse out of two thousand homes and twenty churches have been left standing, untouched. It looks like this is another one for the scientists to solve.'

'This is Ray Brant, from your news helicopter.'

God's Home +